Englis

G000139966

English Popular Education
1780–1975

Second edition of
English Popular Education 1780–1970

DAVID WARDLE

Dean of Teacher Education,
Padgate College of Higher Education

CAMBRIDGE UNIVERSITY PRESS

CAMBRIDGE

LONDON · NEW YORK · MELBOURNE

Published by the Syndics of the Cambridge University Press
The Pitt Building, Trumpington Street, Cambridge CB2 1RP
Bentley House, 200 Euston Road, London NW1 2DB
32 East 57th Street, New York, NY 10022, USA
296 Beaconsfield Parade, Middle Park, Melbourne 3206, Australia

First published 1970
Second edition 1976
Reprinted 1977

Printed in Malta by Interprint (Malta) Ltd

Library of Congress Cataloguing in Publication Data

Wardle, David.
  English popular education, 1780–1975.

  Published in 1970 under title: English popular education, 1780–1970.
  Bibliography: p.
  Includes index.
  1. Education – Great Britain – History.   I. Title.
LA636.W36 1976   370'.942   75–41713
ISBN 0 521 21202 2 hard covers
ISBN 0 521 29073 2 paperback

(First edition ISBN 0 521 08004 5 hard covers
         ISBN 0 521 09631 6 paperback)

CONTENTS

ACKNOWLEDGEMENTS

I wish to acknowledge the assistance of my colleague, Mr C. Barber, in drawing up the chronological table. I also wish to thank my wife for her continual assistance, particularly in the preparation of the manuscript.

PREFACE TO SECOND EDITION

This edition has been brought up to date by the addition of a new chapter describing developments until 1975. The chronological table and list of further reading have also both been revised.

September 1975   DW

PREFACE

In producing this study of popular education in England in the nineteenth and twentieth centuries I have had three main ideas in mind. First, I have attempted to show educational changes in their context. It is impossible to understand educational history unless it is seen as a branch of the much wider study of general history – political, social and economic – if it is treated in isolation it becomes a largely meaningless list of unrelated incidents and although this may provide excellent material for memory training, it is hard to see that it serves any other educational purpose. To take an example, the idea of providing an elementary education for the whole population was first seriously canvassed at the turn of the eighteenth and nineteenth centuries, the period when Sunday schools and monitorial schools first appeared. Why was this so? And, why when faced with the problem of providing mass education, did people turn to schools as the agents of instruction? Schools, up to this time, had by no means enjoyed a monopoly of education. The wealthy favoured private tuition at home, while apprenticeship had been the almost universal method of initiation to trades and professions. If we are to answer these questions we must look outside the rather narrow field of educational history as it is generally interpreted, and consider the assumptions, political or otherwise, which determined men's reactions to events, the political controversies of the time and the social and economic changes which disturbed the existing balance of society. Similarly, if we are to understand the attitude of the state towards education in the nineteenth century it is necessary to seek out the political assumptions which made it impossible for the British government to contemplate a state system of schools like that established in Prussia and France, and to examine the social and economic pressures and the philosophical arguments which progressively undermined these assumptions. In both these cases a student of the history of education is forced, if he is to reach a satisfactory explanation, to probe in some depth into the neighbouring fields of political, social and economic history and the history of ideas.

Secondly, I have tried to make historical experience bear upon contemporary problems. Most students who follow a course in the history of education are not reading history as a main subject and it is not unreasonable that they should be interested in history less as an academic study than for its relevance in the current situation. With this in mind I have been concerned to ask questions about schools, teaching methods and teachers, and about the motives and assumptions which influence educational decisions, and to relate these to contemporary questions, attempting to show why we are faced by these particular problems at this time.

Thirdly, I have concentrated upon asking questions rather than providing answers. This is partly a matter of policy and partly of necessity. In any historical judgment there must be an element of interpretation, and this is affected by the assumptions which the reader brings to the process of judgment. Even where there is agreement upon the facts there may be room for wide differences of interpretation depending, for example, upon the political views of the interpreter. This being so it is important for the writer of a book which is intended mainly for readers who are not necessarily primarily interested in history to be cautious in presenting ready-made answers.

But there is a particular need for caution in this case. The history of education is in a very backward state compared with most other fields of historical study. The facts relating to the development of English education are known in a general way, although there is a depressing shortage of good detailed local studies against which to check the more general works. What is almost entirely missing is a theoretical structure of explanation. Even where we know what happened, we have no very clear idea why it did so. This situation arises very largely from the fact that the history of education has been studied without reference to related disciplines and I have already commented upon the difficulty – perhaps impossibility – of understanding historical changes under these conditions. At the present time the materials hardly exist for any comprehensive explanatory system of theory in the history of education. The important thing to do is to suggest what questions need to be answered by any such theoretical structure, and in the conclusion to this book I have tried to draw out certain questions of this kind and to indicate particular themes or processes of which it seems to me explanations must take account.

D.W.

CHAPTER 1

THE INTELLECTUAL AND SOCIAL CLIMATE OF THE NINETEENTH CENTURY

It was in the last quarter of the eighteenth century that the question began to be seriously mooted of providing mass elementary education in England. I do not propose to discuss here why this should have been the case; this question is considered in chapter 2, but it is relevant to point out that this was a new venture. There was nothing new about the idea of founding charities for educational purposes. This had been a common practice since medieval times and in the early eighteenth century the Society for Promoting Christian Knowledge had been very active in this field. But previous charities had always been limited in scope and it was common for the benefactor to stipulate that the school was for the education of ten, twenty or fifty poor children as the case might be. In contrast, the characteristic feature of nineteenth-century educational charities was that they were general in application, and a serious attempt was made to provide Sunday or day schools for every child in the country. This attempt came within measurable reach of success everywhere except in some large manufacturing towns.

Educational systems do not grow up by mere chance. They reflect contemporary notions about social organization, the nature of knowledge, the possibility of human improvement, the function of government and so on. In this chapter an attempt is made to arrive at the assumptions which determined the response of nineteenth-century people to the social problems of the time. From the point of view of this study the ideas of major thinkers are of far less significance than the construction which quite ordinary people put upon their ideas. Thus it is less important to know what Darwin wrote and thought than what teachers, administrators and school board members understood him to have thought, and they were far more likely to have gained their knowledge of Darwin's ideas by way of Herbert Spencer than from reading *The Evolution of Species by Natural Selection*. Similarly, in more recent times, it is not necessary for our purposes to disentangle the ideas of Dewey from those of his disciples, although Dewey himself, at the end of

1

his career, felt called upon to do this in *Experience and Education*. For the purpose of historical analysis it is convenient to consider intellectual and social movements separately, but it is essential to remember that they did not really occur in isolation and that it was quite possible, then as now for a single person to hold conflicting assumptions without apparent discomfort, and for others, more inclined to introspection, to suffer acutely from the strain of deciding between mutually incompatible courses of action.

The first element to be considered in the nineteenth-century intellectual climate is 'philosophical radicalism', a system of ideas which enjoyed very general assent at the turn of the eighteenth and nineteenth centuries among intellectuals and administrators, and which remained as a major influence upon social and political thinking for the next hundred years. It derived in the first place from John Locke, an English philosopher of the late seventeenth century, whose ideas were developed on the Continent by the French *philosophes*, and returned to Britain at the end of the eighteenth century, when the most eminent exponent of the school was Jeremy Bentham. Bentham was an eccentric recluse who enjoyed a far greater fame abroad than he did at home, but whose teaching was expounded and applied by his many disciples of whom James Mill was perhaps the most distinguished. The ideas of the philosophical radicals, however, extended far more widely than the circle of formal disciples, partly because they fitted very well with the prevailing individualism, and partly because they were capable of presentation in a rather crudely 'commonsense' form, although Bentham himself was an almost impossibly obscure and tedious writer.

From the educational point of view there were four aspects of philosophical radicalism which were particularly relevant. The first of these was the psychology, which derived fairly directly from Locke. The effect of this psychology upon teaching practice is discussed in chapter 5; here we are concerned with its influence upon the provision of education for the poor. It was believed that a person's character and behaviour depended entirely upon experience, heredity being a very minor factor. The mind at birth was *tabula rasa*, a blank sheet, and a child's personality was, therefore, infinitely variable, depending upon his upbringing. It was logical, upon this assumption, to attach great importance to education as an agent of social reform, and to take an interest in measures designed to improve the environment of the poor. The optimistic view that man was perfectible by social engineering, and that human nature was, in fact, improving was shaken by the French Revolution and Napoleonic Wars with their revelation of the extent to which men were still ruled by irrational impulses and susceptible to xenophobic propaganda. But it remained an important element in nineteenth-century thinking, and was reinforced by the scientific advances which are considered later in this chapter.

The second element of philosophical radicalism to examine here is 'utilitarianism'. Thinkers of this school are often referred to as 'utilitarians' because when considering the value of an institution they asked the question, 'what use is it?' The test applied was that an institution, or a chosen course of action contributed to 'the greatest happiness of the greatest number', and 'happiness' was generally interpreted rather crudely as physical well-being. Clearly this was a reforming doctrine and was particularly destructive when applied at the beginning of the nineteenth century to many institutions which had little to recommend them but a long history. The universities, which were in an advanced stage of decay, came in for much criticism from utilitarians, as did the public and grammar schools, the classical curriculum which held the field at that time being an easy target for attack on the grounds of utility.

A third important element in the thinking of the utilitarians was their intense individualism. They took an atomic view of society, the individual being regarded as the basic unit when questions of value were discussed, and the state as merely an assembly of individuals with no organic existence of its own. This attitude was the direct opposite of the position taken up by socialists and communists who laid emphasis upon collective responsibility. Thus Bentham, in his *Introduction to the Principles of Morals and Legislation*, wrote: 'The community is a fictitious body, composed of the individual persons who are considered as constituting, as it were, its members. The interest of the community then is, what? – the sum of the interests of the several members who compose it.'

Enormous importance was attached by the utilitarians to the individual's right and duty to look after his own business, and there was an intense suspicion of interference by the state in private affairs, the sphere of 'private affairs' being very liberally interpreted. This individualism was very deeply ingrained into nineteenth-century thinking on political and social matters, and was one of the chief obstacles to the establishment of a national system of elementary education. It had two aspects. There was a moral objection to interference with a person's affairs. It was conceived to be a man's duty to be responsible for himself and his family, and, although casual assistance by charity or otherwise might be permissible in times of unusual distress, any regular scheme of assistance was thought to be dangerous because it pauperized the recipient and destroyed his sense of independence. Furthermore there was an acute fear of increasing the power of the government by allowing it to assume responsibility for the private lives of its citizens for this was seen as the first critical step on the road to a police state. It was the hallmark of a free country that a citizen stood on his own feet and solved his own problems, even if this involved a measure of hardship in specific cases and a general administrative inefficiency which would horrify a modern civil servant.

If the teachings of this school were accepted there was very little scope indeed for government activity, and this fact was accepted, indeed welcomed by contemporary writers. In his *Manual of Political Economy* Bentham wrote: 'The general rule is that nothing ought to be done or attempted by government. The motto, or watchword of government on these occasions ought to be – Be quiet,' It was statements such as these which led to the use of the phrase 'laissez-faire' to describe the views of the utilitarians upon the functions of government.

Finally in their thinking about education the utilitarians were excessively intellectual. Education was seen as the acquisition of information and rather little importance was given to physical education, imagination, the arts and the emotions. The result is parodied, not altogether unfairly, in Dickens' description of Mr Gradgrind's school in *Hard Times*, and in the field of history rather than fiction the monitorial school was a realization of utilitarian ideas on instruction. This attitude went along with a certain coldness or lack of humanity, which showed itself in a strong tendency to regard people as social statistics. An example of this was the new poor law system introduced in 1834 which was avowedly based upon the principle that life inside a workhouse should be only marginally less unpleasant than starvation outside, since if the workhouses were too attractive the poor would be tempted to live in them rather than trying to remain independent outside. This act reflected the constant tendency of men of this school to think in terms of 'the poor', 'the lower orders', 'the industrious classes' and to forget the individuals who were lost in these generalizations. As was remarked earlier the utilitarians habitually equated 'happiness' with physical well-being and often seemed incapable of realizing that there were other dimensions of human personality. The best known description of this aspect of utilitarianism is J. S. Mill's account, in his autobiography, of his education by his father, James Mill, but the general acceptance of this narrow interpretation of education is shown by the fact that the Edgeworths, whose *Practical Education* revealed remarkable insights into children's interests, displayed great hostility towards aesthetic and imaginative activities, even disapproving strongly of fairy stories for the young.

4

The philosophical radicals were very typical of the eighteenth century in their emphasis on reason rather than emotion. Deep personal involvement in any cause, political or religious was regarded as rather disreputable as it was likely to cloud the cool judgment which was the sign of an educated man. Thus 'enthusiasm' was a rude word with very much the connotation of 'fanaticism', and the Methodists, for example, were described, in an uncomplimentary sense, as 'enthusiasts'. The Romantic movement was a reaction against this attitude of mind, and therefore emphasized everything which the eighteenth century under-valued, personal involvement, emotional expression, intuition rather than cool reason. The paradigm case of a romantic – so typical as to be almost a caricature – was the poet, Byron. He lived at the highest emotional pitch, his troubles receiving the maximum publicity, often by himself. He was constantly at odds with society, the concept of the genius isolated by his supreme talent being a characteristic romantic one. He found a cause to which to dedicate himself in Greek independence. In only one way was he atypical; he had a sense of humour and could occasionally laugh even at himself, which may partly explain why his reputation was higher on the Continent than at home.

The irrational bias which was so strongly marked in romanticism was clearly a reaction against the rather inhuman 'reasonableness' of eighteenth-century thinking; personal involvement and 'enthusiasm' became virtues, and it was creditable rather than otherwise if the commitment came intuitively rather than as the result of long consideration. Of course enthusiasm and a high emotional pitch were not exclusively romantic qualities. They were also characteristic of the Evangelical movement, which is discussed later in the chapter, and was itself a form of reaction against eighteenth-century rationalism. It is important to notice, also, that there were two other aspects of contemporary society against which the romantics and their followers revolted. One was the rise of science and technology which, like utilitarianism, were felt to leave out of account large areas of human experience. Related to this was a protest against the impersonal economic doctrines of the day which were based upon the extreme individualism and denial of collective responsibility which were referred to above.

There were two aspects of romanticism which are relevant in the history of education. The first of these was a nostalgia for the middle ages which continued to be influential throughout the nineteenth century. The effect of this upon literature is too obvious to require comment, but it was also significant in social thinking. One factor in causing this nostalgia was a revulsion against nineteenth-century individualism and a hankering after the medieval feeling of social cohesion.

The medieval town with its gilds and close supervision by the corporation was very different from the sprawling and anonymous industrial town of the nineteenth century and even the feudal system could be thought of, especially at a distance, as an exercise in mutual responsibility. This was one reason why the early socialists showed great interest in the middle ages, William Morris being an obvious example.

Of course it was not merely the attraction of a collectivist society which drew people to the middle ages. Morris and others also drew attention to the impersonal nature of much modern work, arguing that the factory operative had lost the pride in his work which was characteristic of the craftsman under the domestic system. This idealizing of the life of the domestic craftsman, usually conceived of as existing in a golden age vaguely before the industrial revolution, remained until recently a common feature of social and economic history. There was also, no doubt, an escapist element in nineteenth-century medievalism, a desire to brighten up drab modern life with the ritual and pageantry of the middle ages, and, in the intellectual sphere, a desire for the certainties of medieval faith in an age of doubt. It may be that both the last two factors had something to do with the success of the Oxford movement and the revival of Catholicism in the middle of the century.

Romanticism had a strong strain of political nationalism, which is apparent, for example, in Byron and Beethoven. It was in the nineteenth century that the national state began to be looked upon as the standard political unit, and Italy and Germany, for example, achieved national status at this time. The problems involved in nationalism were not really appreciated until the twentieth century. Patriotism was very much a romantic virtue; eighteenth-century intellectuals tended to be internationally minded, and this is not surprising since patriotism involves the sort of emotional commitment – my Country, right or wrong – which was most attractive to the romantic mind and most repulsive, as 'enthusiasm', to the representative of the eighteenth-century 'enlightenment'. When this strong nationalist feeling was allied to the incipient collectivism which was previously mentioned the ingredients existed for the formation of modern totalitarian states, and when both feelings were taken together with the admiration for the romantic hero, as in the writing of Carlyle, the ground was prepared for the popular dictatorship which has been perhaps the typical political pattern of the twentieth century. This is of more than academic interest to educationalists since the spread of romantic views of society had much to do with the slow undermining of the intense individualism of early nineteenth-century England.

A most important factor in the development of popular education in the nineteenth century was evangelicalism. This was the result of the religious revival of the second half of the eighteenth century, combined with a strong sense of social responsibility which led its followers to show a powerful missionary zeal which was criticized as 'enthusiasm' by its opponents. It was from the Evangelical movement that there arose what has often been called the 'Nonconformist conscience', but it is important to notice that the movement was not exclusively Nonconformist and that there was a powerful evangelical wing in the Church of England.

The evangelicals with their combination of social conscience and missionary zeal were a powerful reforming agency. Howard, the prison reformer, Tuke, a pioneer in the provision of hospitals for mental diseases, Shaftesbury and Wilberforce are only conspicuous examples of the reforming efforts of this group, but it is arguable that their best work was done in arousing public opinion so that social reform became a matter of concern among people who had no direct connection with the movement. Evangelicals were active in the early days of popular education, especially in the Sunday school movement. But the influence of this movement in education was perhaps less than might have been expected, perhaps because their interest was essentially in religious instruction and only secondly in secular studies, as a way of acquiring the ability to read the Bible. On the whole, too, the reformers of this school accepted the contemporary social stratification, and were inclined to be suspicious of popular education if carried beyond the rudiments, seeing in it a tendency to make members of the working class discontented with their lot.

The characteristic qualities of the evangelicals, a rather ostentatious piety, strong social conscience, extreme respectability, and a somewhat humourless disapproval of entertainment and pleasure, are also the qualities popularly associated with the typical 'Victorian'. And in this case the popular view contains an important element of truth. Piety and respectability were traditionally middle-class virtues – the strength of puritanism had always lain in the middle class and skilled working class of the towns. Although there were obvious exceptions it was accepted as a general rule that the gentry were, by virtue of their social position, permitted to lapse from respectability, while it was taken for granted that the poor lacked the upbringing and education to enable them to achieve respectable conduct. For very different reasons a surprising amount of drunkenness and sexual irregularity was tolerated among both rich and poor until well into the nineteenth century. One of the social changes which was most obvious both to contemporaries and to subsequent historians was the extension of the middle-class code of respectability and temperance both up and down the social scale. This process began well before the accession of Victoria, but it is not too much of an over-simplification to describe this new tone of society as Victorian. Certainly men like Wellington, Melbourne and Palmerston, who lived on from Regency days into Victoria's reign found themselves in a different, less permissive social climate. The evangelicals had much to do with changing the moral tone of the upper classes, both by their direct example and by their influence upon education. Thomas Arnold, the famous head-master of Rugby, was a good example of an evangelical who was also a member of the Church of England.

The nineteenth century was an age of very rapid scientific and technological advance. Of course the progress made in this period seems slow by twentieth-century standards, but its psychological effect was probably greater than that of the objectively much more dramatic developments of the last seventy years. At the present time people have become accustomed to spectacular advances in man's control of his environment, but in the early nineteenth century such progress was very new. After all the steam railway was the first successful mechanical means of transport. Travel in Europe in the mid-eighteenth century was almost certainly slower than it had been in the time of the Romans. Only in the last quarter of the eighteenth century did rapid improvements in road-making and the design of vehicles bring horse transport to its peak of efficiency, and by the 1840s it was rendered obsolete by the railway. Similarly the sailing ship was perfected in the 1860s when it was already clear that the days of sail were over. Such rapid technological obsolescence is commonplace today but was then a new and startling phenomenon. Historians writing in the 1830s noted with amazement that lace-making machines which had cost £800 a few years before were being broken up for scrap, having been superseded by more versatile apparatus, an event which is nowadays so common that it does not reach the newspapers and certainly not the history books.

These developments produced two contradictory responses which were often to be seen in conflict in the same person. On the one hand was an ebullient optimism, for the scientific advances seemed to bear out the belief of the utilitarians that man could perfect himself by the use of his own mental resources. Human knowledge was being cumulatively increased and with it went a control of the forces of nature which was entirely novel. Wealth from the new industry was increasing as fast as knowledge, and the circle which shared in the distribution of wealth was a large one. Not all the scientific discoveries were related to industry; others directly improved living conditions. Major advances were made in surgery and medicine; after the middle of the century improved public health facilities brought about massive reductions in deaths from epidemic diseases like cholera and dysentery. A new professionalism penetrated even administrative circles. The government became better informed about what was happening through official enquiries and the spread of the civil service. The government also acquired far greater control over events, as is demonstrated, to take only one example, by the progressive intervention of the state in elementary education. As local government, virtually non-existent in the eighteenth century was established over the whole country the traditional anarchy of the large towns was brought under control and important progress made in reducing the amount of crime and vice.

In a different field the increase in knowledge gave men a new understanding of the working of nature. Eighteenth-century thinkers, notably Hume and Kant, had succeeded in establishing the distinction between inductive and deductive methods of enquiry, thus separating science from mathematics, and it was in the nineteenth century that science became a professional pursuit and the boundaries between its existing divisions were mapped out. The physical and biological sciences produced major achievements in this period; the human sciences, psychology, sociology, anthropology showed more promise than performance but even here the work of men like Sir Francis Galton pointed the way towards a scientific study of human behaviour. The most cautious man might reasonably feel that there was a movement towards a better understanding of man and his environment.

This optimism which is often taken as being characteristic of the Victorian period was reinforced by the fact that, by comparison with the eighteenth century, the nineteenth was remarkably free from major wars. Between 1815 and 1914 European wars were short and localized and the casualty lists short by Napoleonic standards, negligible compared with the Thirty Years War of the seventeenth century in Germany or with twentieth-century World Wars. It was not unreasonable to hope that the world was moving towards a time when war would be obsolete and international disputes settled by discussion. Certainly a nineteenth-century Englishman was rather unlikely to have any personal experience of the effects of war. At the same time there was room for a liberal to feel optimism about the political scene. At home there was a progressive widening of the franchise and constitutional movements among the working class became strong and effective in the second half of the century. Disabilities upon Catholics and Protestant Dissenters were removed. The corruption, intimidation and irrelevant revelry endemic at elections of every kind died out as the century went on. On the Continent the great multi-racial empires were visibly tottering and national states were being carved out of them. There was a tendency, rather hesitant it is true, towards the formation of parliamentary regimes. There was much to be done, but the movement was in the right direction; rationalism and liberalism seemed to be leading Europe towards a period of peace, toleration and free trade.

But there was also a profound Victorian pessimism. The advance of knowledge undermined existing beliefs, and values. The classic example of this process, of course, was the work of Darwin, but the whole intellectual atmosphere of a period of rapid scientific progress was uncomfortable for people who sought for unquestionable foundations upon which to base their beliefs for it was the basic axiom of the scientific method that no assumption was unquestionable. Once again the impact of this new spirit was particularly severe upon men of the nineteenth century who could look back at close range upon a period before the accepted beliefs and values had been called into question. It was in the 1850s that the clash between science and faith reached a climax and it was no longer possible for intelligent men to ignore the issue. By this decade historical criticism of the Bible, which may be traced back at least until the 1670s had begun seriously to shake the fundamentalist position, but far more alarming was the assault of scientists upon the account of creation contained in Genesis. The critical point concerned the mutability of species. The biblical account plainly stated the species had been created in their modern form, while science favoured a process of evolution. By 1857 Charles Lyell and his followers from the side of geology and Darwin and others from the side of biology had reached the point where they could explain the evolution of species in purely scientific terms. In Chapter Five of *Father and Son* Edmund Gosse describes the acute dismay of his father, a distinguished naturalist, when he was forewarned by Darwin of the impending publication of his theory. This chapter remains perhaps the best brief account of the agony of a scientist who was also a fundamentalist Christian when faced with the necessity 'to stand emphatically in one army or the other'. Tennyson and Matthew Arnold were other men from the first generation of the age of doubt, and, particularly in the poetry of Arnold, one can recognize the post-Darwinian man hankering after the assured faith of his father.

There were other reasons for intelligent men to feel reservations about the tendency of contemporary developments. It seemed to some that there was a more rapid scientific than moral advance; man was gaining control over his environment, but not over his own nature. It was left to the twentieth century to demonstrate conclusively that science and technology could be used at least as efficiently in the interests of destruction as of construction, but it was already apparent by the 1830s that industrial development might involve, might even depend upon, a vast and ruthless exploitation of the poor. In the same way it dawned upon some people that the establishment of large national states, while in keeping with liberal political doctrines, might represent a major threat to world peace, not to mention national security. The question arose, for example, whether the appearance of a united Germany was necessarily to be classed as 'progress' if the new state followed a foreign and domestic policy of the kind initiated by Bismarck.

Two side-effects of the scientific revolution of the nineteenth century are of particular significance in this context. The first of these was a quite new popular acceptance of the idea of 'change' as being something likely to be good in itself. It is a fair generalization to say that until the nineteenth century the concept of 'change' was related to that of 'decay'. There was an inbuilt suspicion of projects to alter existing institutions which inevitably made the task of a reformer extremely difficult. At the present time 'change' is more nearly related to 'progress' or 'reform' so that if one speaks of 'social change' it is assumed that one is advocating some form of betterment of social conditions.

In the nineteenth century this development did not proceed very far. The bulk of the population remained intensely conservative and acceptance of change as good in itself was limited to a small, if influential class. It is only in quite recent times that innovation has come to be generally, and usually uncritically, welcomed. Firms no longer make a point in their advertisements of being long established; they rather prefer to emphasize the modernity of their products. Similarly a modern government must be seen to be active in introducing new legislation. It is no longer acceptable, as it was in the nineteenth century, for even a Conservative government to have no programme other than managing the day-to-day business of administration and dealing with problems as they arise.

This acceptance of innovation arose from three sources. One was the utilitarian belief in human perfectibility which has been previously discussed, and which obviously involved a willingness to countenance programmes of social and political reform. But important contributions came from contemporary developments in philosophy and science. From the German philosopher G. W. F. Hegel was taken the notion of historical determinism. History was seen as a dialectical process, developing in stages. Each stage contained within it the seeds of the next, and development from one stage to another was inevitable. Thus, to take an example from Marx, who was a follower of Hegel, history passes from feudalism through capitalism to socialism. In its passage from Hegel and

Marx to popular acceptance the belief in historical determinism underwent an important change. The original argument was that to oppose the historical process was futile since events were determined by, for example, economic pressures. But it was very easy to slide from the statement that opposition to change was futile to the statement that opposition to change was morally wrong, and this transfer of meaning was generally, if unconsciously, made. It is doubtful if historical determinism made much impression in England in the nineteenth century; in the twentieth, however, it has contributed powerfully to the development of a situation in which the word 'reactionary' carries definite overtones of moral disapproval.

More influential in the nineteenth century than historical determinism was the acceptance of the theory of evolution. In the popular interpretation at least, evolution was taken as being a movement towards improved species. One spoke of species as being 'higher' or 'lower' on the scale of evolution, and for the layman it was difficult to use such terms without tones of approval or disapproval creeping in. An important implication of evolutionary theory was that the process of evolution was still continuing, and it did not seem unreasonable that man should assist the process by judicious manipulation of the environment.

The second by-product of nineteenth-century scientific advance was that scepticism became a popular frame of mind. As has so often been the case, although the questioning of old certainties began in the nineteenth century the full force of this development has been felt in the twentieth. From the educational point of view it is important to notice that scepticism may lead to two very different results. It may lead to acceptance of the scientific attitude, which may be summed up by saying that while certain assumptions must be made in order for enquiry to proceed, no assumption is absolute and unquestionable. On the other hand it may lead to irrationalism. Confused by a situation in which the individual has to establish his own standpoint amongst a clash of authorities, people may decide that, since no authority can establish his case beyond dispute, and since personal decision is worrying, they will commit themselves uncritically to the discipleship of some charismatic leader who promises to do their thinking for them and to deliver the answers. The popular dictators who have been so numerous in the twentieth century have derived much of their support from this feeling, and it seems probable that the fashion of the last few years for mystical Eastern religions is an example of the same phenomenon.

The nineteenth century was an age of much increased social mobility. This was due partly to the spread of consciously egalitarian doctrines and partly to the industrial revolution, which necessitated a large increase in the geographical mobility of labour, and at the same time threw up many new occupations which could not be classified in the existing social structure. This phenomenon produced the same ambivalent response as the scientific revolution; some people took an optimistic view, some were pessimistic; many were both at one time or another. There were two reasons for optimism. Some people welcomed the decreasing rigidity of the class structure as a sign of the approach of an age of equality and universal brotherhood, when social distinctions would be a thing of the past. More common, certainly among the upper and middle class was approval of the new tendencies as heralding the appearance of the 'meritocracy'. Such people accepted the existence of social distinctions but believed that they should be based upon other criteria than birth. Alternative tests of merit which were frequently advocated were the accumulation of large sums of money as proof of success in business, and the passing of competitive examinations, which was taken as proof not only of intellectual prowess, but also of administrative ability; the competitive examination became something of a cult in Victorian times. Obviously this was a point of view very popular among self-made men, and the Victorians had an immense admiration for hard work and the self-made man, but it could also be adopted for different reasons. In the second half of the nineteenth century men with a knowledge of foreign affairs were much concerned about the challenge to British supremacy which was offered by France, Germany and potentially by the United States, both in the industrial and military spheres. Such men were much struck by the great reserves of manpower possessed by these countries, and realized that, since Britain's population was relatively limited, it must be used efficiently if the country was to compete with a reasonable chance of success.

These arguments naturally led people to take an interest in education, particularly in technical training, but they also led them to advocate that the search for talent be carried on throughout the whole population and not limited to that small proportion which could afford to make use of the public and grammar schools. They therefore applauded the appearance of a social structure which made it easier for the able children of poor parents to rise through effort and educational qualifications to positions of influence and responsibility.

Other people found the phenomenon of social mobility frightening. Some, for example, took the view that what was valuable in the culture of a society is preserved by a highly educated minority and that a lengthy liberal education was necessary for the appreciation of 'culture' – the word being used here in an aesthetic rather than a sociological sense.

They regarded the extension of mass elementary education with suspicion on the grounds that such education, because of the limitations of time and expense, must be a poor imitation of that given to the cultured few, and that those who passed through the schools would acquire little understanding of genuine culture. They further feared that in an egalitarian state the values of the cultured few would be swamped by those of the semi-educated masses. Such people found some justification in the quality of the popular press which arose in the late nineteenth century as mass literacy was brought about by universal compulsory education, and maintained that a golden age of folk culture had been destroyed by the industrial revolution and was replaced by the age of pre-digested popular entertainment. There was a quite unhistorical idealism about these arguments. The descriptions of the pre-industrial revolution folk-culture left out the sordid side, the traditional drunkenness of the English craftsman, the immense popularity of bear-baiting, cock-fighting and public executions. But the elitist critics of egalitarian doctrines did have a point. The advocates of the new democracy did depend to a remarkable extent upon a quite uncritical belief in the ability of the semi-educated man to voice an intelligent opinion on matters where the experts were in doubt. In view of the terrifying ignorance and brutality of a substantial proportion of the population of Victorian England it was not unreasonable for even benevolent men to have reservations about the spread of egalitarianism. After all the most recent experience of the effects of this doctrine, in the French Revolution, had not been encouraging either to democrat or conservative, and the utilitarian belief that human nature could be infinitely varied by social engineering was a largely untested assumption. If education and associated social reforms failed to civilize the lower classes the outlook for popular democracy was gloomy.

This attitude could have either a political or a cultural aspect. Some people were alarmed at the prospect of rule by the masses; others were afraid of the dilution of culture. Both groups agreed that the masses required leadership which must be supplied by some form of elite. Clearly the dispute between the elitists and the egalitarians had important implications for education. The egalitarians leaned very heavily upon the ability of mass education to raise the general cultural level of the population; the elitists denied that education could do this, or at least argued that only a minority had the intellectual endowment and could spend the time upon the kind of education necessary to produce a cultured person. If the educational facilities of the country were disposed upon too wide a front the educational standard of the population would not rise but fall since there would be an inadequate concentration of teaching power upon the really talented few who should be the scientists, poets and artists of the next generation. In the modern phrase, 'more means worse'. This argument, of course, is still with us; much of the current dispute about the expansion of higher education depends upon the question whether a university education is seen as the normal conclusion to a course at secondary school, or whether it is seen as a stage in the production of an intellectual elite.

It was pointed out earlier in the chapter that at the beginning of the nineteenth century public opinion was strongly opposed to state intervention in anything which could be construed as the private affairs of the individual. This attitude of mind was, of course, a major obstacle to reform, and one of the most important developments of the century from the point of view of the history of education was the progressive abandonment of this doctrine of 'laissez-faire', and the corresponding acceptance of collectivism as a respectable political doctrine. This has now reached the stage where, for example, it is thought quite reasonable to propose that the government should legislate to prevent the smoking of cigarettes because of their danger to health, a suggestion which would have been almost incomprehensible to the Victorians who, in the interests of individual freedom, declined to prevent parents from dosing their infants with dangerous drugs such as opium.

Laissez-faire was challenged first in the field of practical social problems and as early as the 1830s and 1840s it was coming to be recognized that there were grave difficulties in the way of its consistent application. It was not until the 1880s, however, that political philosophers, of whom T. H. Green was probably the most important, worked out a rationale to support systematic state intervention in social matters.

Individualism, for fairly obvious reasons, had always been a philosophy which appealed more to the well-to-do than to the poor; it was clearly to the advantage of the factory owner that trades unions or other associations of working men should be prohibited, that taxation should be low and that restraints on trade should be reduced to a minimum. The working class, on the whole, had always favoured collective security and they continued to do so, often to the exasperation of political economists who taught that competition and the survival of the fittest was the natural state of man. This was a point upon which, judging by contemporary writers, there was almost complete mutual incomprehension between the classes. Throughout the nineteenth century working men produced friendly societies, co-operative societies and trades unions, while middle-class observers were perpetually surprised by the amount of mutual support they discovered among the very poorest workers particularly in times of distress. In speaking of laissez-faire, therefore, we must notice that although it enjoyed wide currency among influential classes, it was never a universal creed.

By the 1830s its application was causing grave concern and doubts were freely expressed about whether a policy of complete non-intervention by the government was really as fair as it appeared at first sight. Such a policy required that all members of society be treated as autonomous units and that no discrimination be exercised by the government in favour of any class. Leaving aside the fact that much nineteenth-century legislation was manifestly discriminatory against the working class, it soon appeared that there were certain groups in society who could not be described as autonomous in any meaningful way. Slaves and children were obvious examples, and it proved to be necessary for the state to step in and protect them against exploitation. But legislation for such groups generally affected other groups as well. This was conspicuously the case with the factory legislation of the 1830s and 1840s. Here it proved to be impossible to limit the hours of work of children without also limiting the hours of the adults who worked with them, so that the government found itself interfering, accidentally but none the less effectively, in relations between management and labour.

At the same time it became apparent that, even in relations between adults, for the government to pursue a policy of non-intervention often meant, in practice, favouring one group at the expense of another. Thus the pure theory of laissez-faire rejected collective bargaining by workmen on the grounds that it was a limitation of the free right of contract between individuals; a workman should be free to sell his labour where he pleased, and an employer to hire labour where he pleased. Unfortunately this apparently equitable arrangement worked out greatly to the advantage of the employer. He could offer terms to one workman, and, if he refused the terms, in the absence of a system of collective bargaining, another workman would soon be found who would accept them. The choice before the workman was to accept the employer's terms or to face unemployment, and since in a laissez-faire economy there was no unemployment pay, this could mean starvation or, at the best, the miseries of the workhouse. The workmen understood very well their individual weakness when opposed to the employer, which explains their efforts, throughout the nineteenth century, to form strong trades unions, and when working-class political parties arose at the end of the century they had a strong collective bias.

It was at this point that laissez-faire came under attack at the philosophical level. The attack centred upon the utilitarian view of society as made up of atomic individuals who were necessarily in a state of competition, and the point was made that the utilitarians thought in terms of the 'abstract individual', whereas, in fact, man was always a member of society and could only function as a human being within society. From this it was argued that freedom must be thought of in its social context; mere freedom to do as one wished involved the freedom of the strong to exploit the weak, and this meant that the weak enjoyed no freedom at all. T. H. Green suggested that the answer lay in the concept of 'positive freedom', which made it the duty of the state to intervene actively to allow every citizen the freedom to use his talents in the common interest. In a lecture delivered at Leicester in 1881 he spoke as follows:

If I have given a true account of that freedom which forms the goal of social effort, we shall see that freedom of contract, freedom in all the forms of doing what one will with one's own is valuable only as a means to an end. That end is what I call freedom in the 'positive' sense, in other words the liberation of the powers of all men equally for contributions to the common good . . . Our modern legislation then with reference to labour, and education, and health, involving as it does manifest interference with freedom of contract, is justified on the ground that it is the business of the state, not indeed directly to promote moral goodness, for that, from the very nature of moral goodness it cannot do, but to maintain the conditions without which a free exercise of the human faculties is impossible.

The criticism of Green and other members of the school which is generally called 'idealism', involved a flat rejection of the premises upon which laissez-faire was based. This is apparent when we see Green using phrases such as 'the goal of social effort' or 'contributions to the common good'. But these ideas provided a rationale for a policy of positive activity by the government at a time when people were already much concerned about the practical results of the negative role enjoined upon the government by laissez-faire thinking.

The development of English popular education was inevitably affected by the assumptions and preconceptions which are discussed in this chapter. The effects of developments in philosophical, psychological and political views upon the curriculum, for example, are considered in chapter 5. It may be useful to conclude this discussion with a few instances of the very direct bearing which factors such as these can have upon educational institutions; the list is not, of course, comprehensive but merely suggestive.

The strong relationship between elementary education and the Church is a feature of English education which arises from the conditions under which mass schooling for the poor was instituted. On the one hand was a government firmly wedded to a policy of non-intervention in social matters and quite unready to take the same sort of initiative as the Prussian and French governments took in the early years of the nineteenth century. On the other hand was the Evangelical movement with its strong missionary zeal to save the souls of children from 'Satan's strongholds' in the manufacturing towns. In the individualistic climate of the time it was virtually inevitable that elementary schooling should remain as a subject for charity and that it was only late and reluctantly that a national system of education was introduced.

Given the fact that a state system was out of the question in the early nineteenth century, cheapness was bound to be of the utmost importance in elementary schooling, and one has to look no further for the reason for the enthusiastic welcome given to the monitorial school. Of course it had other attractions. The division of labour and the mechanical organization appealed to businessmen and industrialists who saw in it the factory system applied to education, the minute sub-division of subject matter conformed to the psychology of the day, and the intense emphasis on competition and emulation fitted in well with the individualism of the utilitarians.

The history of popular education in England is closely bound up with the progressive abandonment of individualism and the corresponding acceptance of collectivism. This is a point which will be emphasized elsewhere in the book and it is only necessary here to draw attention to three landmarks in the involvement of the government in popular education. The first direct effective intervention by the government in elementary education was in the 1830s, when the Treasury grant for school building was introduced. Significantly this occurred at a time when a new government, elected after an extension of the franchise with a mandate for reform, was showing itself aware of the practical difficulties involved in the application of laissez-faire principles. The Treasury grant was accompanied by the first effective factory act, by a new poor law and by the abolition of slavery within the Empire. In the same way the reorganization of elementary education in the period 1906 to 1914, which involved a liberalization of the curriculum and important developments in welfare and medical services and the education of handicapped children did not occur in a vacuum. The government in office was a Liberal one, coming to power after a long period in opposition, and with conditional support from the Labour party, effectively represented in Parliament for the first time. Quite apart from its work in the educational field this government passed important social legislation which may be regarded as the foundations of the welfare state. To bring the account up to date the 1944 Act was passed in a state of public opinion which applauded the Beveridge Report and the establishment of the welfare state proper, while the now famous Circular 10/65 was despatched by a government which quite avowedly proposed to use comprehensive schools as an instrument for social levelling, and which saw itself as entitled to use the power of the central government to force local education authorities to fall into line with its policy.

CHAPTER 2

RECURRENT REASONS FOR EDUCATIONAL EXPANSION IN ENGLAND

Education is not an activity upon which governments are naturally inclined to spend money. It is only quite recently, historically speaking, that the idea of government provision of educational facilities has seemed reasonable. It has always been seen as the parents' responsibility to bring up their children, and, although governments have fairly frequently felt called upon to remind parents of their duties, they have been reluctant to proceed any further in the matter. Even today expenditure upon education is certain to be cut at any sign of financial crisis.

It is not difficult to see why this is so. Schooling is an expensive process and the results are delayed and difficult to assess. A government which proposes expenditure upon education is, in effect, taxing one generation for the benefit of the next, and if the taxpayers are to accept such a burden they need to be very strongly persuaded of its necessity.

It is sometimes pointed out that England was very late in establishing an official system of schools compared with, for example, the United States or some of the European powers, notably France and Prussia, and the conclusion is drawn that lack of interest in education is a curiously English phenomenon. It is doubtful whether this is true. A more likely explanation of England's very slow start in national organization of education is that the country did not experience certain pressures which forced other states into educational activity. In France, for example, the establishment of a system of elementary schooling was related to the military needs of the Napoleonic Empire and the same motive was equally apparent in the reorganization of Prussian education after the humiliation of defeat by the French in 1806. The aim in both cases was not simply to train potential soldiers, but to turn out good Frenchmen or Prussians imbued with the proper social and political attitudes; the schoolmaster was not so much a drill-sergeant as a propagandist, although the values to be inculcated included an admiration for martial success as well as a respect for political superiors.

In the United States of America there was a different reason for government interest in education. The USA were, of course, free from fear of foreign invasion in the usual sense in the nineteenth century, but they did experience an invasion of a kind, an invasion of masses of immigrants, from every country, very many speaking no English. If America was to remain a nation the children of these immigrants had to be turned into Americans, and this gave a particular urgency to the extension of education. It also gave American education a consciously nationalist flavour which some English commentators have found objectionable.

So far we have considered motives which have led to forms of education which aim at conformity. But it is possible for a country to emphasize the importance of education because of the value it places upon individuality. An important element in those versions of Christianity which stem from Calvin was the ability of the individual to commune with God, and to read and interpret the Scriptures for himself. Clearly if this personal religion were to be a reality then popular education was of great importance. On the other hand literacy was of less moment in those Roman Catholic and Anglican communities where it was accepted that it was the function of the clergy to interpret religious matters to the laity. It may be for some such reason as this that Scotland and the Netherlands were among the first countries to establish effective systems of public education.

In general, therefore, any society needs to be strongly motivated if it is to take a collective interest in education, but it happens that at the turn of the eighteenth and nineteenth centuries, public opinion in England was particularly opposed to any intervention by the state in the private affairs of citizens. This was the period of 'laissez-faire', when the doctrine was generally accepted that 'that government is best which governs least'. The functions of the government were considered to be substantially restricted to foreign affairs and to keeping order at home – 'order' being interpreted in the most liberal manner – and it was only rather grudgingly admitted that assistance might be given to people who, for one reason or another, were incapable of helping themselves, paupers, lunatics and the like. Even in these cases it was believed that there was a moral danger in extending assistance too far since the assisted people, through becoming accustomed to receiving assistance, might lose their habits of self-reliance, and it is almost impossible to overemphasize the importance attached by nineteenth-century Englishmen to self-reliance, an importance which shows very clearly in Victorian adventure stories for boys. In such stories there is, almost invariably, a scene in which the hero stands up to, and thrashes, the bully. For the hero, however small, to complain to authority of bullying would be unspeakable cowardice.

There were good historical reasons for the almost universal acceptance of this apparently callous attitude. The seventeenth century had been a period of paternal government and Englishmen were very conscious that they had only narrowly avoided an autocracy of the Continental type, exemplified in the popular mind with the French monarchy which had just collapsed in the excesses of the French Revolution – an object lesson to all good Englishmen. The events leading to the 'Glorious Revolution' of 1688 had given the English an intense suspicion of government, and the government itself, whether Whig or Tory was absolutely opposed to suggestions for state control or even state intervention in citizens' affairs. Education was regarded as peculiarly a matter for private enterprise because the possibilities for political indoctrination were fully appreciated and government control of schools was seen as the hallmark of the 'police state'.

From another point of view self-dependence could be looked upon as a cardinal virtue. It is very difficult for modern people to realize just how little government there was in the early nineteenth century. There was no police force and no way of keeping public order unless there were really serious riots when the military could be called in, but this almost invariably meant loss of life, and magistrates were honourably reluctant to proceed to such lengths. Besides there were never enough troops to deal with all emergencies. Social services such as hospitals, dispensaries, alms-houses were non-existent unless provided by charity. Unless one was prepared to accept the humiliation of going 'on the parish' there was no alternative to self-reliance.

For a variety of reasons, therefore, the English have been historically reluctant to accept a national system of education and public opinion has had to be profoundly stirred before important advances in the direction of such a system could be made. In the present chapter it is proposed to examine certain factors which periodically recur to bring about such a stirring of popular interest in education.

The most pervasive of these recurrent motives for educational activity is the call for 'social discipline'. At times of rapid social change people often feel that a moral decline has set in, that the lower orders, or the young no longer know their place and are disobedient and lacking in respect. Established systems of values are being challenged and the social order is in danger. Under these circumstances education is called in so that the young may be inoculated against the contagion of subversive doctrine and made into pillars of the establishment. Such education has always, in the past, been aimed at the children of the poor, and has, very naturally, emphasized the importance of contentment with one's station in society and of a sober and industrious life.

This motive has a long history. Elizabethan and Stuart legislators were much exercised in their minds about the problem of unemployment and an act of 1576 empowered magistrates to establish workhouse schools 'to the intent that youth might be accustomed and brought up in labour and then not likely to grow to be idle rogues'. This act led to sporadic attempts by magistrates and town councils to establish spinning schools which were to pay for themselves by the profits of the children's labour. Far more significant, however, were the efforts of the Society for Promoting Christian Knowledge, which led a campaign for the establishment of charity schools in the early years of the eighteenth century. Many hundreds of these schools were founded and some continue at the present day. The larger of these charity schools not only provided a free education but also apprenticed their alumni and provided them with a uniform, so that they were popularly known as 'Bluecoat' or 'Greencoat' schools.

At the end of the eighteenth century various circumstances led to another surge of interest in mass education as a cure for social problems. England was experiencing the early effects of the industrial revolution and one of these was the appearance of large industrial towns like Birmingham, Leeds and Manchester. These towns gave a new dimension to the problem of poverty. Until this time, except in London, the poor had been scattered over the whole country a few in every village; now huge numbers of working people swarmed together round the new industries and in times of unemployment their destitution was terrifying or tragic according to one's point of view. Whatever one's political persuasion it was, at any rate, impossible to ignore the vast slums which grew up round the major cities and which served to keep the misery and threat of the poor constantly before the eyes of influential people.

Furthermore this new urban proletariat lay quite outside the existing social and political organization. Some of the industrial towns were entirely new – Birmingham was an example – and there was no local authority higher than the parish. Others were historically important, like Nottingham, but in these the municipal authorities were frequently quite indifferent to the social problems that were appearing within their nominal jurisdiction, for local government shared with national government in a decline in energy and confidence due to the 'laissez-faire' doctrine. It is a debatable point whether the lives of the urban poor were any worse, physically or spiritually than the lives of the poor had always been but people were disturbed and frightened by their vast numbers and by the patent lack of any administration to control them or provide social services for them.

A confusing factor was that many of the new workmen were engaged in trades which had no place in the traditional social structure. The relative status of craftsmen and the various grades of shopkeepers was clearly understood, but where did engineers fit in? Or operatives in lace factories? These trades fell outside the apprenticeship system, which was moribund by the end of the eighteenth century, and the situation was further complicated by the decline of previously respectable occupations like that of hand-loom weaving. At all points in the social scale there was uncertainty about status, and therefore a tendency to take status seriously and to attempt to define the privileges and obligations of one class in relation to another.

There were, therefore, reasons for concern about the way in which accepted social patterns were being disturbed. But the disturbing factors which have been discussed so far were impersonal, the result of major economic changes. There were, however, current political doctrines which were avowedly subversive of the existing political and social structure, and the results of these doctrines were to be observed in France. It is difficult to exaggerate the effect of the French Revolution upon English social and political thinking. In its early days it was greeted with approval – rather patronizing approval since it was believed that France was moving towards an English constitutional monarchy, but this attitude completely changed until by the time of the 'reign of terror' and the execution of the King and Queen, events in France were regarded as a terrible warning of the dangers of 'democracy' and mob rule. Known radicals like the scientist Joseph Priestley, suffered for their opinions and even Pitt, a reforming prime minister, moved towards reaction. Reform of Parliament, hardly even a controversial measure in 1790, was abandoned and was not taken up again for forty years.

For all these reasons people were concerned about the security of the social system and they turned to education as an instrument of social regeneration. It was believed that subversive ideas could best be combatted by taking the children and inoculating them by a course of schooling. In the 1780s the Sunday School movement became immensely important, and when one day's education per week was found to be inadequate people looked for a way of providing day schools. The monitorial system, which enabled one teacher to supervise the work of a large number of children – the more the better according to the inventors of the system – provided a solution to the great problem facing sponsors of elementary schools, finance. Within a few years monitorial schools were active all over the country and societies had been established by Anglicans and Nonconformists to further the cause of popular education which became a fashionable subject, enjoying Royal patronage.

The motives of the protagonists of popular education were clearly stated. In 1810 the aims of the newly founded national school in Nottingham included teaching reading and writing and 'accustoming the children to habits of cleanliness, subordination and order'. Ten years later Samuel Wilderspin's infant school aimed at 'The cultivation of their morals and the preservation of their health . . . the promotion of mutual affection and social harmony, personal cleanliness, becoming manners and due subordination'. But the ideals of this movement were most explicitly and succinctly stated long afterwards by Robert Lowe in a pamphlet he wrote in 1867:

The lower classes ought to be educated to discharge the duties cast upon them. They should also be educated that they may appreciate and defer to a higher cultivation when they meet it, and the higher classes ought to be educated in a very different manner in order that they may exhibit to the lower classes, that higher education to which, if it were shown to them they would bow down and defer.

Of course this argument in favour of educating the poor was two-edged. On the one hand it could be argued that 'the educated mechanics are better conducted in all that relates to their social duties, more refined in their tastes, and more guarded in their language than the uneducated', but there was an equally good case for maintaining that instead of inculcating 'due subordination' education might have the highly undesirable effect of making the poor question the necessity of their poverty. It is interesting to find that in this case reactionary thinkers were in complete agreement with working-class leaders about the effects of education, for it was an important part of the doctrine of the 'moral force' wing of working-class political movements that ignorance was the great ally of oppression.

The establishment of the monitorial schools was by no means the last occasion upon which social discipline has been urged as a reason for educational development. In the 1880s there was much concern in the large towns about the 'street corner hooligans'. This represented an early form of a very modern problem – the rational use of leisure. In Victorian towns there was absolutely no form of recreation outside the public houses which were incredibly numerous and, as social standards rose, philanthropists were disturbed by revelations of bestial drunkenness and brutality. In Nottingham in 1850 there were 193 inns and ale-houses, one for every 250 people. The YMCA and working-men's clubs were early attempts to provide alternatives to the ale-house and the street corner. In the 1880s there was an active movement led by the Recreative Evening Schools Association to persuade school boards and other interested parties to establish evening classes in activities likely to appeal to young people with no academic ambitions. In 1889 a report by the Nottingham School Board summed up the aims of the new evening schools:

If we can win our young people from the corners of the streets and from the byways and alleyways into our schools and they can there learn *not to forget* what the country has paid so much for them to learn, we shall have accomplished a great and good work. Our aim is not so much to gain government grant as to win our young people to a better and nobler life, and so . . . the moral advantages to the individual student and to the community at large are more than we can measure.

The report went on to make 'a most confident appeal to all who desire less crime and poverty, quieter streets, more self-respect and more respect for others, to give us their sympathy and support'.

More recently still public concern over juvenile delinquency or 'the revolt of youth' has led to demands that schools should exercise their socializing function in the interests of conformity.

The demand for political discipline is very difficult to distinguish from the demand for social discipline and for most purposes it is not necessary to do so. Indeed they are often merely different aspects of the same attitude of mind. Both often show a strongly authoritarian bias, and from the political point of view it is natural that this bias should manifest itself at the time of the French Revolution in a call for education – perhaps indoctrination might be a better word – to combat dangerous egalitarian doctrines and teach respect for political betters.

But the call for political education can be given a more generous interpretation. It is a sensible assumption that one of the requirements for the success of a political democracy is an educated population and it is not mere coincidence that the progressive expansion of the franchise was accompanied by the spread of education. The first grant of public money for education in 1833 immediately followed the passing of the first Parliamentary reform act and it was the next extension of the suffrage, in 1867, which prompted Robert Lowe's celebrated observation, 'We must compel our future Masters to learn their letters'. Forster's Education Act of 1870 provided the framework for a national system of elementary education and two measures of 1876 and 1880 made elementary schooling effectively compulsory. But perhaps the best expression of this motive for educational expansion occurs in the speech by H. A. L. Fisher, introducing the 1918 Education Bill to the House of Commons:

We are extending the franchise. We are making a greater demand than ever before upon the civic spirit of the ordinary man and woman at a time when the problems of national life and world policy upon which this House will be asked to decide have become exceedingly complex and difficult, and how can we expect an intelligent response to the demands which the community propose to make upon the instructed judgment of its men and women unless we are prepared to make some further sacrifices in order to form and fashion the minds of the young . . .

A new impulse was given to this motive for educational expansion in the period between the World Wars by the rise of new totalitarian states, of which Nazi Germany may be taken as a typical example. It was observed that these states made use of propaganda and indoctrination on a massive scale to produce a docile, unquestioning population, often employing the new mass media with terrifying success. It was believed that an educated population was less susceptible to propaganda and that, therefore, education was a defence against the spread of dictatorship. The same argument has frequently been advanced since the Second World War, and certainly receives some support from the fact that opposition to autocratic government finds its traditional strength in the intelligentsia and student population. Both fascist and communist governments have found it necessary to expend much effort on muzzling intellectual criticism by censorship or by more drastic measures, and both have made great use of the education system for political indoctrination, laying stress on starting the process as young as possible when the children are most suggestible. An interesting modern variation on the use of education as an inoculation against propaganda is the suggestion that the critical capacity produced by education might render people less vulnerable to the pressure of advertising.

So far we have considered the demand for political education *for* the working class, but such education may also be demanded *by* the working class, and in this case the motive may be rather different. From the early years of the nineteenth century working-class political movements tended to have two wings. On the one hand were those men who favoured violent methods of changing the political situation, including, in extreme cases, revolution. Typical of this way of thinking were the 'physical force' Chartists led by Fergus O'Connor in the 1830s and 1840s, and much later the Bolshevik wing of the Communist party. The opposition favoured a policy of 'gradualism', of working within the constitution for reform rather than revolution, and their programme was based upon the idea of demonstrating that the members of the working class were respectable and responsible and that it was manifestly unjust that they should be excluded from political power. The 'moral force' Chartists led by William Lovett were early examples of this movement, and in the second half of the century the various groups which coalesced to found the Labour party were of this persuasion. In Russia the 'physical force' Bolsheviks were balanced by the 'moral force' Mensheviks.

It was very natural that the 'moral force' elements in working-class movements should lay great importance on education as a way of demonstrating the readiness of working men for political power, particularly since members of the 'establishment' were themselves committed to the belief that educated working men were socially and politically reliable. Both sides, for rather different reasons, were agreed that in mass education lay the best hope of averting the fear of 'the red peril' which had reached panic point at the time of the French Revolution and had been revived in 1848 when huge Chartist demonstrations had coincided with violent revolutions all over Europe. Thus 'moral force' Chartists founded adult schools, debating clubs and libraries, some of which survived for many years after Chartism disappeared in 1848, while the 'Fabians' particularly concerned themselves with political education. The Workers' Educational Association and Ruskin College were products of the continued interest of the 'moral force' party in education at the beginning of this century, and from 1916 onwards the Labour party was committed to a policy of secondary education for all.

It was not only the working-class leaders who saw education as a political weapon; the campaign for the emancipation of women was accompanied by a demand for the expansion of women's education. The university extension movement of the 1870s and 1880s received much of its impetus from the demand by women for an education of genuine academic content and many of the men and women who were concerned in founding secondary schools and colleges for women were also active in the emancipation movement.

Perhaps the most popular of motives for educational expansion at the present time is the need for scientists, technologists and technicians to meet the requirements of industry, and, in particular, those industries which contribute to the export market. In fact the need for industrial training was one of the original reasons for the establishment of an educational system in England, because from the middle ages until the eighteenth century the great majority of people acquired their education through apprenticeship. In theory apprenticeship provided more than merely vocational training because the apprentice lived with the master who was responsible for his moral development as well as his technical competence, but in later days, certainly, the requirement of residence was frequently neglected and it seems likely that the moral supervision was more of an ideal than a reality. Nevertheless, even in the nineteenth century when apprenticeship had declined, there were cases of masters who took their responsibilities seriously and interested themselves in their apprentices' general education. William Felkin, a Nottingham businessman who wrote extensively on education in the middle of the century recorded that his master, Nathan Hurst, encouraged his early literary efforts:

as several of us (apprentices) were fond of literature ... it was his frequent custom, while our work was done, to ask what works we were reading, what we thought of them, and to throw out ideas, often of value in drawing attention to important or difficult points, or aiding to form a correct estimate, or helping to make the best of what we read ... By this a stimulus was given to the first employment of my pen in writing some short papers to be read and discussed at the weekly meetings of seven apprenticed youths held in the schoolroom and supplied with dim tallow candles, barely sufficient to make the manuscript legible.

Against this can be set the following complaint which was made in 1626 about the ill-treatment of an apprentice by a master, a rather interesting case because the apprentice was a girl; it does not seem to have been unusual to indenture girls, generally in various forms of needlework:

hee hath beaten her in her head most greeviously sundrie times. Moreover hee hath beaten her upon the face, which were most greevious that she had almost lost one of her eyes. Since that time he hath beaten her and punched her with his fiste upon her syde, that she was scarce able to get her wind. What by him and by her she was so beaten and pinched upon her armes dyvers tymes that she were so black it would pittie anye Christian to beholde. Hee hath beaten her upon her face that hee hath made her bite her lips with her owne teeth. When theire hath been her brother and other to intreate and speake in her behalfe, they hath spoken she should be the vilder and worse used for theire speeches.

By the end of the eighteenth century apprenticeship had declined as a method of technical training, partly because of the appearance of new skills which were outside the old industrial organization and partly because this organization of gilds, companies and corporations had shared in the general decline of administrative energy which characterized the eighteenth century. The period of the early industrial revolution in England, from the middle of the eighteenth to the middle of the nineteenth century saw surprisingly little interest in technical education and nothing was done to revive or replace the moribund apprentice system which lingered on very largely as a euphemism for sweated child labour. There were several reasons for this. In the first place it is possible to exaggerate the amount of technical innovation and mechanization which occurred at this time. The demand was less for technicians than for unskilled workers to undertake jobs which in a genuinely mechanized industry would be performed by machines. This explains the high demand for the labour of children who could carry out simple, repetitive tasks at a rate of pay which no adult would accept. Those technical inventions which were made generally came from amateur inventors, of whom Sir Richard Arkwright, originally a barber, is the archetype. Many of these men, Macadam and Stephenson were examples, were not only without technical training but had no formal education at all, and they were inclined to share the impatience of the self-made man for institutional education. Much later in the century Samuel Smiles, biographer of the 'Great Engineers' still believed that engineers were born rather than made and that technical training was of little value. Such views, reinforced by the long-lived English love of the amateur found additional support from the 'laissez-faire' doctrine which taught that education was very much a personal affair, and that it was certainly not the duty of the state to interest itself in the matter.

The lead of the English in industry and commerce in the early nineteenth century was so overwhelming that industries could continue in their own way without fear of foreign competition and with little concern for design or efficiency. The Great Exhibition of 1851 was held in the Crystal Palace in Hyde Park, which was, fittingly, designed by an amateur, Sir Joseph Paxton, a gardener by trade. The exhibition was planned to demonstrate to the world the glories and triumphs of British industry and commerce, and this it did, almost every prize being taken by British individuals and firms. However, amidst the self-congratulation there were influential voices raised to point out that there were warning signs. Certain other countries, notably Prussia, France and the United States, although only just beginning to industrialize, were doing so in a disturbingly professional manner and with threatening results. It was seen by the more critical spectators that in some respects, especially in design, foreign goods were improving far more rapidly than English manufactures and threatened, in the immediate future to surpass them. This situation was attributed by almost all experts to the extent and efficiency of secondary and technical education in these countries which contrasted very markedly with the parlous state of English secondary schools. An immediate result was a tendency to take education seriously as a national investment and, in particular, the Science and Art Department was founded to encourage, through advice and financial assistance, technical education, with particular emphasis on design and craftsmanship.

The Paris Exhibition of 1867 confirmed the relative decline of British industries and underlined the lesson that the rapid progress of Continental countries was due to the superiority of their design and to their more efficient use of manpower, both arising from extensive provision of secondary and higher education. It is significant that three great enquiries were held in the sixties – the Newcastle, Clarendon and Taunton Commissions – which examined English primary and secondary education, and although the results were disappointing, the investigations do reflect contemporary concern about the backwardness of English schools. It is also interesting that repeated enquiries, notably the Taunton, Cross and Bryce Commissions looked to Prussia – which became Germany in 1870 – for guidance. There were special reasons for this as will be suggested below, but certainly these enquiries were influenced by the highly organized state of German education and industry and their close and conscious interrelation.

It is hardly necessary to point out the importance of this motive in the 1970s. Since 1945 there has been an increasing tendency to look upon education as a national investment – it has always been thought of as a personal investment – and since 1945 a whole series of reports and white papers have driven home the need for 'educated' or 'scientific' manpower, always comparing the situation in England with that obtaining in USA, USSR, Germany and Japan among other countries. It is only necessary to mention that since the Second World War there has been the Percy Report of 1945, the Barlow Report of 1946, a report of the National Advisory Council on Education in Industry and Commerce in 1950, White Papers in 1956 and 1962, the Robbins Report of 1963 and the Dainton Report of 1968. The list alone indicates the pressure for the expansion of technical education which has built up during the period.

Of course it is not necessary to suppose that there is universal agreement about the need for technical education. The industrial training boards, set up as a result of the White Paper of 1962 have often received a tepid or even hostile reception from both sides of industry, and it is well known that the need for training for teaching is regarded with suspicion by people both inside and outside the profession. The point is that there is a powerful body of opinion which supports the expansion of education on the grounds that the country, in order to remain competitive must invest in education to provide scientifically and technically trained manpower.

When one studies the development of the English educational system one is surprised to discover how often important stages in the development are closely connected, in time at least, with wars. This connection is sufficiently marked in the nineteenth century but becomes much more obvious in the twentieth, and it is worthwhile examining this curious relationship to see if any suggestions can be offered about why it should occur.

The first attempt in England at the provision of day schools for the mass of the poor was made at the height of the Revolutionary and Napoleonic Wars with the monitorial schools introduced by Joseph Lancaster and Andrew Bell. There were several reasons why this attempt occurred at about this time, some of which have been discussed in this chapter, but the fact remains that the Napoleonic Wars, in their early stages at least, were ideological contests and one motive for the establishment of these schools was certainly to attempt to unify the different social classes against the dangerous doctrines of the Revolution. At precisely the same time the French were organizing their education with the avowed intention of strengthening and consolidating their national power. The Prussians, too, after the defeat by the French in 1806 selected the education system as the basis of their national recovery.

There was a lengthy period of international peace after the end of the Napoleonic Wars in 1815 but the third quarter of the century produced a crop of wars which had a bearing on educational development. The Crimean War of 1854–6 was notable for its revelations of the incompetence of British officers and it is not unreasonable to connect these revelations with the contemporary commissions of enquiry at Oxford and Cambridge and the appointment of the Clarendon Commission to investigate the public schools. More important, however, were the successes of Prussia against Austria in 1866 and France in 1870–1 and of the North against the South in the American Civil War. In both cases it was believed that a critical factor in the success had been the higher level of education reached by the rank and file soldiers as well as the more professional attitude of the officers. In the same way that educated men were believed to make efficient workmen, they were believed to make efficient soldiers, and by 1870 informed opinion in England was becoming concerned not only about the country's relative economic decline but also about its political situation, particularly in view of the tendency towards the formation of powerful national states in Europe, the recent appearance of Italy and Germany being in everyone's mind. In his preliminary speech W. E. Forster explicitly stated this as one of the motives behind the introduction of the 1870 Education Bill:

Upon this speedy provision of education depends also our national power. Civilized communities throughout the world are massing themselves together, each mass being measured by its force; and if we are to hold our position among men of our own race, or among the nations of the world we must make up the smallness of our numbers by increasing the intellectual force of the individual.

For precisely the same reasons the French, after the disasters of the Franco–Prussian War, undertook a major reorganization of their education under Jules Ferry.

It is difficult to say whether the passing of the 1902 Education Act was influenced by the Boer War or not. Probably other factors were far more significant, although the war did have the important effect of underlining Britain's political isolation and thereby giving added force to Forster's warning about the efficient use of our small numbers. But there was one by-product of the Boer War which had important and far-reaching results in the field of education, and which, in fact, led to a considerable widening of the scope of public education.

Throughout the nineteenth century recruiting surgeons had complained about the quality of the recruits they were called upon to examine. In 1845 a surgeon in Birmingham remarked: 'the working men are small, delicate, and of very slight physical power; many of them are deformed too, in the chest or spinal column'. He added that of 613 recruits only 238 were fit for service. But war did not make a great impact on Britain in the nineteenth century. What campaigns did occur were on a small scale and fought by professional soldiers. The Boer War, however, received immense publicity because of the recent improvements in communications and large numbers of volunteers were called for. Public opinion was profoundly shocked when it was revealed just how poor was the physical condition of many of the recruits. One result was a surge of interest in physical education; a symptom of this was that from 1906 elementary schools were allowed to hold organized games in school hours. In 1908 the Boy Scout movement was formed, led by Baden-Powell one of the heroes of the Boer War, and the Girl Guides followed two years later. There was another important aspect to this concern about physical welfare, however. Along with a call for physical training and rational recreation went a demand for the introduction of measures to improve the living conditions of children and to provide medical services available to the poor. In 1906 a Liberal government was returned to Parliament with a mandate to carry out substantial measures of social reform and some of these were of particular significance to children. These included permission for local education authorities to spend money on medical services and school meals, and important legislation about child labour and the treatment of delinquent children.

33

Further evidence of the effect of war upon provisions of this kind can be seen in the fact that between 1939 and 1945 the number of children receiving school dinners at subsidized prices rose from 130,000 to 1,650,000. In the same period the proportion of schoolchildren receiving school milk rose from 50 per cent to almost 100 per cent.

The Boer War was the last of the nineteenth-century wars; the First and Second World Wars were entirely different in nature and their effect upon social conditions far more dramatic. Both wars gave a great impulse to industry; there was full employment and high wages and an urgent interest in technical efficiency. There was therefore a demand, both from the armed forces and from industry, for educated men and women so that a secondary or higher education became an attractive investment just at the time when, because of high wages, more people were in a position to afford such education for their children. This is reflected in the fact that between 1914 and 1921 the proportion of elementary school children proceeding to secondary schools – grammar schools in modern terminology – rose from 53 per thousand to 97 per thousand.

A more important factor was that both wars were 'total' wars. The whole nation was involved. Armies were enormous and compulsory service spread the military burden over every class of the population. Industry was mobilized, there was direction of labour and rationing brought the reality of war to the people at home. In the Second World War in particular, aerial warfare made it dubious whether it was more dangerous to serve at the front or to remain in England. The air raids of the First World War were less destructive but their psychological effect was perhaps as great because of their novelty. The result was a very strong feeling of national unity and a reluctance to return to the social divisions of pre-war days. At the same time it was felt that those who had fought in the war deserved to return to 'a world fit for heroes to live in'. The casualties in these wars were so great that Forster's words about the importance of educated manpower for national security were given redoubled force. This was perhaps particularly the case during the First World War, partly because the British battle casualties were so terribly high, and partly because the war followed a hundred years without a major war. G. A. N. Lowndes, in the *Silent Social Revolution* mentions a case of a school from which 720 old boys died, leaving only 80 sons, and figures like this caused people to think about the value of children as a national investment.

For all these reasons the wars produced a surge of interest in social reform, and, as part of this, in educational expansion. H. A. L. Fisher, introducing the 1918 Education Bill, said:

A third feature in the movement of opinion is the increased feeling of social solidarity which has been created by the War. When you get Conscription, when you get a state of affairs under which the poor are asked to pour out their blood and to be mulcted in the high cost of living for large international policies, then every just mind begins to realise that the boundaries of citizenship are not determined by wealth, and that the same logic which leads us to desire an extension of the franchise points also to an extension of education.

A symptom of this way of thinking was the setting up of a Ministry of Reconstruction in 1916 and practical results were an extension of the franchise in 1918, the establishment of the Ministry of Health in 1919 and the Education Act of 1918. Unfortunately many of the measures proposed by this Act were victims of the economic troubles of the inter-war period.

The same factors which had given to politics between 1914 and 1918 a certain magnanimous and forward-looking character operated again from 1939 to 1945, and on this occasion they were reinforced by the experience of evacuation which made many people aware for the first time of the conditions under which slum children lived. Once again there was a tendency to look forward to and plan for a better world after the war, and once again this feeling issued in much legislation, which, taken together, form the basis of the 'welfare state'. It is particularly significant of the climate of opinion that a considerable proportion of this legislation was passed by a coalition government with a powerful Conservative majority. Examples are the Town and Country Planning Act and, especially relevant here, the 1944 Education Act. In fact interest in education did not finish with the 1944 Act; two commissions reported on technical education in the next two years.

So far we have considered the positive results of war upon education, but it is possible for war to inhibit educational advance. The short term effect of modern war is generally disastrous. Large numbers of teachers, often the younger and more energetic, are removed for war service, school buildings are commandeered and new building stops, evacuation may cause widespread confusion, the demands of the armed services and of industry prevent young men from taking up higher education. By the end of a war of five or six years buildings and equipment, which have not been properly maintained or replaced are in a decrepit condition. But the cost of war is perhaps more serious in the long run than the temporary check caused by war conditions. The appointment of the Newcastle Commission and the subsequent institution of 'payment by results' in 1862 were directly due to the expense of the Crimean War and caused a major set-back in the development of elementary education. The World

35

Wars of the twentieth century were vastly more expensive, and the economic troubles which have plagued Britain for the last forty years are due, in part at least, to this expense. The effect on education has been to nullify the plans made during the war-time periods of idealism. The provisions of the Fisher Act of 1918 almost disappeared in the slumps of the 1920s and 1930s under the economies of the 'Geddes Axe' and the May Committee. The raising of the school-leaving age to fifteen years, for example, was not implemented until after another war and another education act. Compulsory attendance at continuation school, allowed for by the 1918 Act, and frequently recommended since, never has been implemented. Raising the age of leaving to sixteen years, stipulated in 1944, has only been put into effect a quarter of a century later. In general, therefore, the effect of war upon educational expansion is complex, and perhaps more conspicuous in idea than in fact.

There is one very important factor leading to educational expansion which stands by itself, very different from the others. All the factors discussed so far have been external to the educational system. Certain social or political developments have disturbed influential people or sections of the population who have reacted by adopting a favourable view towards investment in schooling, and the raising of educational standards. One of the most striking phenomena in the history of education in England in the last hundred years, however, has been the way in which provision of education at one level has led in due course to a demand for education at a higher level. This is a recurring process, internal to the educational system and apparently largely independent of external conditions, and it has been one of the major forces, although an almost unrecognized one, leading to the expansion of secondary and higher education.

This factor first becomes apparent in the 1880s. When the school boards assumed their responsibilities in 1870 their first tasks were to provide schools and to compel children to attend them. These tasks occupied the attention of even the most go-ahead boards throughout the 1870s. Children were reluctant to attend and parents reluctant to send them; an average attendance of 65 per cent of the roll was about the norm and the level of attainment in the schools was miserably low. The order of priorities is demonstrated by the fact that the Nottingham School Board, one of the most enlightened and progressive in the country, paid its school attendance officers £20 per year more than a qualified teacher. By 1880 the battle to get the children into school had, by and large, been won; average attendance was of the order of 90 per cent and, although schools were still plagued by part-time attendance of older pupils, the situation had been reached when, for the first time, the great mass of the child population attended school regularly for six or seven years.

Immediately the schools encountered a totally novel problem. The more intelligent or more highly motivated children proceeded rapidly through the schools, and since, by the requirements of the grant earning regulations they had to be raised a standard each year, they arrived at the top standard before they were due to leave and had nowhere else to go. The Education Department went some way towards meeting this situation by instituting another standard, the seventh, but children continued to reach this either at an age when they could not leave or to find that their parents wished them to stay on to improve their education. Naturally the larger school boards, faced by a large number of such children, struck, apparently independently, Bradford being first in the field, upon the idea of gathering them together into one school for more advanced work. These schools were known as 'higher grade' schools and were soon doing recognizably 'secondary' work leading to examinations such as the Oxford and Cambridge 'locals' and the London matriculation. The question then arose whether such schools were eligible for government grant, which was payable to elementary schools under the terms of the 1870 Act. The importance of this dispute in this context is that in 1870 no-one had thought it necessary to specify the upper limits of 'elementary' education; the lower limits had seemed more relevant. The rise in the standard of work and the consequent demand for secondary education was completely unexpected and the Education Department was never able to arrive at a satisfactory answer to the dispute which was one of the prime reasons for the 1902 Act.

The appearance of the higher grade schools was due entirely to internal pressure and not to campaigns by citizens stirred to action by fear of commercial competition or political danger, although the value of the schools was soon realized by such men who became their enthusiastic supporters. The same phenomenon precisely occurred after the 1902 Act which instituted a rigid distinction between secondary schools with a literary curriculum on the one hand and elementary schools on the other. In 1907 a regulation laid down that grants would only be paid to secondary schools if they made 25 per cent or more of their places available, without fee, to children from elementary schools, to be selected by examination. There was no means test attached to this rule; any child, from an elementary school, who qualified was entitled to a free place. It was assumed, quite reasonably in the circumstances of 1907, that no parent who could afford fees would send his child to an elementary school. But by the late twenties pressure upon secondary school accommodation was so intense that middle-class parents were sending their children to elementary schools in order that they might qualify for 'free places', and one of the economies introduced in 1930 by the May Committee was to insert a means test into the regulations so that 'free places' became 'special places'.

At the same time local education authorities were finding the demand for advanced work from elementary school pupils so great that they were once again experimenting in the field of secondary education with 'senior' schools and 'central' schools. The impression is gathered from some histories of education that the idea of secondary education for all was pioneered by the Hadow Report of 1926 but, in fact, this report recorded the fact that pressure for recognizably secondary education was intense and publicized certain suggestions for meeting the demand.

Since 1944 the phenomenon of the autonomous expansion of education has been familiar in both secondary and higher education. This topic will receive special attention in chapter 8 so it is sufficient here to point out that every attempt to predict future demands in these fields has fallen ludicrously short of the truth and that the largest demand, especially in higher education, has not always appeared in those subjects which offer the largest vocational advantages, a fact which suggests that other than economic factors are at work.

In a historical analysis of this kind there is a danger of suggesting artificial distinctions. It is, therefore, important to notice that the factors which have been distinguished rarely function quite independently. Normally two or more work together and it is difficult, and perhaps unnecessary to disentangle their effects. For example, in wartime a feeling of social unity and a wish to make a better world after the war may give rise to idealist plans for future educational developments which may well be supported by a call for social discipline arising from revelations of slum conditions produced by recruiting, evacuation or bombing. At the same time fear of ideological subversion may lead to a call for political education on the lines of the 'know your enemy' campaign run in the forces during the Second World War. These positive factors may be balanced by wartime disorganization and a call for financial stringency.

In such circumstances it is misleading to isolate one particular factor unless the existence of the others is borne in mind. Perhaps two main points emerge from this discussion. In the first place educational expansion occurs for a number of reasons which inter-react in complicated ways, and any attempt to follow these reasons up at all adequately must lead deeply into social and political history. The

Recurrent reasons for educational expansion

educational system does not exist and change in isolation. Secondly, the same factors constantly recur with minor differences and in different combinations so that a knowledge of past problems is relevant to those who have to solve present problems.

CHAPTER 3

THE RAW MATERIAL

In the first two chapters we have discussed the assumptions with which
people approached the problem of popular education, and some of the
motives which impelled people to turn their attention to the problem. But
this discussion has so far been conducted in the abstract, so that, to take
an example, although it has been pointed out that the demands for the
re-establishment of social and political discipline were powerful motives
leading to the establishment of elementary schools in the early nineteenth
century, nothing very concrete has been said about why this motive
should be so powerful at this time. It is now necessary to attempt some
description of the circumstances under which the members of the
working class lived in the period from about 1840 to 1870. This
particular period is selected since by 1840 England was recognizably an
industrial country – it was at the census of 1851 that the urban
population first exceeded the rural population. The social and economic
problems which are associated with the industrial revolution were by this
period fully developed, but there was not yet anything which could be
termed a system of education and the state had not yet begun to interfere
in any very effective way by social legislation. It is hoped that this
examination will cast some light upon the difficulties which faced the
teachers and managers of elementary schools when they attempted to
spread the rudiments of education over the whole population and will
also help to explain why the country moved reluctantly but progressively
towards a state system of elementary education. It may also provide
a foundation for an estimate of the results achieved by that system.
For obvious reasons this chapter will concentrate upon the lives of
working-class children, but some attention will also be given to the
lives of adults, partly because the quality of life enjoyed by an
adult will have an important bearing on the lives of his children,
partly because contemporary opinion looked upon elementary
education principally as a crusade directed towards saving children
from the lives led by contemporary adults. It was also tragically
true that working-class children began work so early that the dis-

tinction between childhood and adulthood lost much of its meaning.

Before embarking upon this study one or two preliminary points require to be cleared up. First, there is the difficult question of precisely who constituted the working class, and what proportion of this class could be considered as likely to form the clientele of public elementary schools. This is complicated by the fact that these schools, which started under the stigma of being charity schools, became significantly more popular as time went on and their standard of work rose, so that the higher grade schools of the 1880s and 1890s received much support from families which a little earlier would have patronized private schools of the intermediate or 'writing school' class. It is noticeable that this class of private school became almost extinct in this period. In the period from 1840–70, however, it remained generally true that one did not send one's children to a public elementary school if one could afford the fees of a respectable private school. These fees were not very high; a school which charged 9*d.* per week in 1870 was taken as lying above the reach of the families who would send their children to board schools, and there were many schools which charged fees of up to 2*s.* or 3*s.* per week which drew their children from families which were definitely 'working class'.

Nevertheless it is possible to specify within reasonable limits that very numerous class of society whose children might be expected to attend public elementary schools, and which therefore falls within the limits of this study. E. J. Hobsbawm quotes an authority of 1867 who estimated[1] that 77 per cent of the 24 million inhabitants of Great Britain fell into the 'manual labour' class, which was narrowly defined to exclude all shop-workers, shop-keepers, foremen, supervisory workers, etc. Of these, 15 per cent were considered as forming a kind of aristocracy with wages of 28*s.* to £2 per week which contrasted sharply with the 10–12*s.* per week which was the miserable average pay of the unskilled workers who formed more than half of the working class. At the time of which we are speaking this aristocracy of labour, together with the 'white collar' workers would be unlikely to make use of public elementary schools preferring the private schools which have been just mentioned. They therefore fall outside our terms of reference, but it will be necessary to pay occasional attention to their activities since, as an educated, articulate and politically conscious minority they were natural leaders of the working class. They also provided support for the various attempts at the provision of adult education which were made both for and by the working class in the nineteenth century, the Mechanics' Institutes and University Extension being the best known examples.

[1] E. J. Hobsbawm, *Industry and Empire* (Weidenfeld and Nicolson, 1968), p. 128.

This chapter, therefore, is concerned in the main with the living conditions of those members of the working class who cannot be classed with the aristocracy of labour, and in the middle of the nineteenth century this meant at least four-fifths of the whole class. But it is important to remember that even when, for our purposes, this minority of highly skilled and relatively highly paid men is excluded, the working class formed an extremely heterogeneous body. There were very large variations in income and in degrees of comfort from the unskilled labourer, whose income, marginal at the best of times, was peculiarly susceptible to fluctuation through the casual nature of his trade, to the man who was on the border of the fortunate 15 per cent. The only common factor in this very large group was the ever present possibility of complete financial disaster through unemployment – and the trade cycle was a familiar phenomenon at this period – injury, disease or just old age. Where the mother of the family was working, and this was usually the case particularly in those industries where the factory system had been established, even a confinement could mean a major crisis, not only because of the new mouth to feed but because of the mother's loss of earnings. The hard fact was that at any time between 1830 and 1850 there was an absolute minimum of 10 per cent of the whole population who were paupers. It was the declared policy of the poor law authorities that life in the workhouse should be 'less eligible' than the most unattractive employment outside, and families entering the workhouses were divided, men, women and children being housed separately. The working of the poor law was a cause of the most bitter resentment among the working class, but a member of the semi-skilled or unskilled majority was rather fortunate if he avoided asking for relief at some time or another. As late as 1900, of the worst paid 40 per cent of the working class, two-thirds became paupers during their life.

But there were distinctions within the working class, as in any class, which did not depend upon financial variables. Among the casualties of the industrial revolution were many skilled craftsmen whose trades were rendered obsolete by technical innovations, hand-loom weavers and framework-knitters for example. The incomes of these men declined until they were surviving in the most terrible poverty but they still retained some of the pride of skilled men, reinforced by the fact that many could remember a time when they had been independent masters, or at least enjoyed a measure of semi-independence. A symptom of their attitude of mind was that they were significantly more interested in education than the bulk of semi-skilled and unskilled men, many of whom earned better incomes. At the beginning of the nineteenth century indeed, there were several framework-knitter poets. None were of any great literary merit, but men of this kind moved at a level well above that of bare literacy, and in this respect showed their relationship to the aristocracy of labour of which mention has been made.

It is necessary to make one other preliminary observation. The period from 1790 to 1850 was one of continuous social and political unrest. The line between the working class and the upper and middle classes became more distinct; resentment and demands for redress of grievances and for political power on the one hand were met by fear and repression on the other. After 1850, however, relations between the classes became less strained. Working-class political movements turned away from 'physical force' towards 'moral force' and there was little of the violent protest, sometimes highly organized, sometimes merely despairing, which had been endemic in the earlier period. This change, which was commented upon at the time and has been confirmed by later research, was clearly related to the long period of general prosperity which followed 1850. So far as the working class was concerned this prosperity was very relative, but there was less of the grinding and hopeless poverty which was so common in the first half of the century, while there was also a slow but definite improvement in the conditions of life in the large industrial towns.

With these warnings against the dangers of over-hasty generalization we can turn to examine the problems which faced the elementary school teacher and his managers in the middle of the nineteenth century. Their first problem was the condition of the children when they entered school. They had been brought up in an environment in which education, however generously that term may be interpreted, simply had no place. They were not merely ignorant; they were totally unequipped to begin the process of learning. Sir James Kay-Shuttleworth described two types of child to be found in elementary schools. The first was from the rural manufacturing areas of the West Riding:

They probably have never lived but in a hovel, have never been in a street of a village or a town; are unacquainted with common usages of social life; probably never saw a book; are bewildered by the rapid motion of crowds; confused in an assemblage of scholars. They have to be taught to stand upright – to walk without a slouching gait – to sit without crouching like a sheepdog. They have to learn some decency in their skin, hair and dress. They are commonly either cowed and sullen or wild, fierce and obstinate. In the street they are often in a tumult of rude agitation.

Children from the East End of London presented other problems.

A different kind of brutishness is shown by a large class of scholars living in the most degraded parts of great cities. A London child, living in a street of brothels and thieves' dens with parents living abandoned lives, spends his days in the Kennel among sharp-witted restless little creatures like himself. He is his own master. His powers of observation are singularly acute; his powers of decision rapid; his will energetic. He is known as 'the arab of the street'. He learns a great deal of evil. Perhaps he is an accomplished thief or beggar, or picks up a precarious living by holding horses, sweeping a crossing or costermongering.

When children of this kind were brought into the schools they presented the teacher with appalling problems since a lengthy socializing process had to be undertaken before anything remotely like academic work could be begun, and little or no co-operation was to be expected from the family. G. A. N. Lowndes describes one such group of children.[1]

They were a wild lot gathered in the Willow Alley shed. Not one boy had experienced any but parental discipline before, and most of the little fellows had been used to blows. When the teacher spoke to a lad the youngster's hands were instinctively made ready to protect the head. Their minds were in a turmoil; their curiosity was at fever pitch. Some were hardy enough; some were very intelligent in appearance; some were cowed and sly but vicious; some were dulled into semi-imbecility by hunger, disease, ill-usage. They had no conception of the meaning of an order, and the teacher was obliged to drill them again and again in the simplest movements. The power of paying attention was almost wanting in them. So far as attainments were concerned the boys were tolerably level. Not one knew the entire alphabet and those who had picked up a slight idea of the letters from the street hoardings were decidedly vague. The teachers found it impossible to interest them in any subject for more than five minutes. They had the fluid mind of the true barbarian and it was quite useless to attempt any species of coercion.

But the teachers' difficulties did not stop here. Their efforts to overcome their pupils' initial handicaps were largely defeated by irregular attendance, by the probability that pupils would be withdrawn for long periods when business was good and the demand for child labour was high, and by the early age at which children finally left school. Most schools had schemes for the award of small prizes or privileges for regular attendance but it was the unusual school which secured a daily attendance of 75 per cent of the children on its rolls, while there was nothing that a school could do to prevent children being taken away to work when still very young. Unless a pupil remained as a monitor or pupil-teacher he was extremely unlikely to stay after the age of ten years. In 1842 one elementary school master informed the Children's Employment Commission that 'the boys leave school generally at a very early age; on an average they do not remain more than twelve months. At this

[1] G. A. N. Lowndes, *The Silent Social Revolution* (O.U.P. 1937), p. 16.

time the number on the books is 120; in the last twelve months 112 have left the school'. Another master remarked

> the boys who attend are from six to ten years of age: there are very few above that age. The number in attendance greatly fluctuates, which witness attributes to this being a manufacturing town. During the last twelve months about 340 boys have on the whole been in the school, so about 120 have gone out. They are withdrawn from the school on the average at nine to go to work. A large number, however, leave earlier to go as seamers or runners. Some have left for this purpose as young as seven. If trade is good the number in attendance is considerably diminished.

Inevitably the school life of even a pupil who attended regularly was extremely short. There was very general agreement with the calculation of an inspector who, in reporting to the Committee of Privy Council on Education, estimated the average school life as being rather under two years.

Under the circumstances it is not surprising that the academic standard achieved by public elementary schools was dismally low. When they tested reading in inspected schools, Her Majesty's Inspectors were in the habit of dividing the pupils into four classes. The first class read 'letters and monosyllables', the second class read 'simple narrative', the third read 'in the Holy Scriptures' and the fourth class read 'books of general information'. In other words only the fourth class were fully fluent and able to use their reading to any effect. In 1847 the inspector for the Midland area reported that 'out of 12,786 who were present at the examination, I find that 2,891 can read the Scriptures with ease, and that 651 can read books of general information with ease and fluency'.

So far as writing was concerned it almost always got no further than copy-writing, usually on slates. Almost no pupils left elementary school able to employ their writing skill independently. Another HMI, writing in 1845, reported that,

> of the 13,381 children who were examined in reading three out of every eleven were writing on paper. This writing upon paper I found in every case to consist of simply imitating in their copy books, copies set them by the master, or copy slips. In no single instance did I find that the children had been practised in writing upon paper otherwise than in imitation of the models thus constantly set before them.

In noting the unimpressive performance of these schools it is important to remember that the inspectors only saw those schools which applied for grant, and that by and large these were the better schools. If the non-inspected public elementary schools and the cheap private schools had been taken into account the achievement would have appeared even more depressing. But added to this was the fact that a large proportion of the children of poor parents never attended school or did so with such irregularity that their attendance was insignificant. Reliable statistics of school attendance covering the whole population for this period are non-existent, but it seems probable that from one-third to one-half of the working-class population had not attended school for a significant period. School attendance was generally worst in the large towns, partly because such areas naturally tended to have large populations of the very poor and partly because they found difficulty in raising the necessary money to establish and maintain schools. Even when schools existed they were rarely filled. When the school board was instituted in Nottingham in 1871 and carried out a detailed survey it found that there were places for upwards of 12,000 children, but that only 7,000 were even nominally in attendance. Perhaps the greatest single handicap to progress in the elementary school in this field was the absence of any system of compulsion, since from this sprang the whole complex of problems related to the short school life and irregular attendance.

The result of numerous enquiries into the educational condition of the children of the poor at this period may be summed up in the words of a sub-commissioner who collected evidence for the Children's Employment Commission of 1842:[1] 'With respect to the children and young persons who came under my observation, I should fail in my duty if I did not state that, in the aggregate they are entirely destitute of anything that can be called, even allowing the utmost latitude to the expression, a useful education.'

It has been mentioned that the circumstances under which the children of the poor were brought up left them not only ignorant but also unequipped for the process of education. What, then, were the conditions of life of the poor at this time?

The first point which strikes any investigator in this field is the perfectly staggering child mortality. There were enormous variations from place to place and between social classes, but the figures for the healthiest areas showed that 28 per cent of all children were dead before they were five years old. In Rutland, for example, a healthy rural area, in the 1840s 2,865 children out of 10,000 died by the age of five years. By

[1] *Children's Employment Commission, 1842*, Appendix Part I, p. 35.

contrast, in Leeds, 5,286 children out of 10,000 died by the same age. But even these figures do not reveal to the full the disadvantage of being born into a family living in the slums of an industrial town since variations between the best and worst wards of the same town were very great. In 1845 the percentage of children who died before the age of four years in different wards in Nottingham was as shown in the table below.

Ward	Percentage of children dead before four years
Park	28·8
Sherwood	31·8
Castle	33·9
Exchange	39·7
St Mary's	35·3
St Ann's	42·3
Byron	44·5

Twenty years later the position was no better. The Children's Employment Commission of 1862 produced figures showing how many deaths occurred in each ward and how many of these deaths were of infants under one year of age. In Park Ward 98 out of 734 deaths were of infants – about 13·3 per cent. In St Ann's Ward the number rose to 558 out of 2,138, a proportion nearly twice as great; while in Byron Ward one-third of all deaths – 501 out of 1,507 – were of infants. Terrible as they are, these figures do not tell the whole story because it was common knowledge that a significant number of deaths, especially those of illegitimate children were concealed. It is a fact that in industrial towns fewer than half of all children of the poor born alive survived to the age when they might be expected to begin school, and that, although the position was not quite so bad in rural areas the infant mortality rate still remained appallingly high.

It is not surprising that those children who survived the perils of infancy frequently did so in a sickly and delicate condition, and reference has been made in the first chapter to the concern frequently expressed about the physical condition of the working classes by recruiting surgeons and others who had reason to pay particular attention to the facts. It is very difficult to separate the effects of early environment from the enfeeblement caused by incessant hard labour from too early an age, but from a combination of causes members of the working class aged very rapidly and were seldom to be found at work beyond what would now be considered middle age. Friedrich Engels writes as follows:[1]

The men wear out very early in consequence of the conditions under which they live and work. Most of them are unfit for work at forty years, a few hold out to forty five, almost none to fifty years of age . . .

Of 1,600 operatives employed in several factories at Harpur and Lanark, but 10 were over 45 years of age; of 22,094 operatives in diverse factories in Stockport and Manchester, but 143 were over 45 years old. Of these 143, 16 were retained as a special favour and one was doing the work of a child. A list of 131 spinners contained but seven over 45 years, and yet the whole 131 were rejected by the manufacturers to whom they applied for work, as 'too old', and were without means of support by reason of old age!

The effects of an upbringing such as that received by the children of the urban working class in this period are further demonstrated by the average age of death of members of different classes in various parts of the country. An investigation carried out in 1842 produced the results shown in the table below.

	Gentry	Tradesmen	Labourers
Rutland	52	41	38
Truro	40	33	28
Derby	49	38	21
Manchester	38	20	17
Bethnal Green	45	26	16
Liverpool	35	22	15

There were obviously several factors at work here. The gentry would benefit from the best medical attention, the best diet and better housing and sanitation. The variation between town and country, which has been observed before in connection with infant mortality, must be attributed to the fact that whatever the hardships of the rural worker – and they were many – he at least avoided the over-crowding, the epidemics and the filth of the urban slums. But care must be taken not to idealize the life of the rural population, even in contrast to that of the urban proletariat. The first half of the nineteenth century was a miserable

[1] F. Engels, *The Condition of the Working Class in England in 1848* (Allen and Unwin, 1892), pp. 159–60.

period for the farm labourer. There was even a labourers' revolt in 1830 and the industrial towns were constantly supplied with labour by a massive emigration of farmworkers who could no longer find a living in their home villages.

The depressed physical state of working-class children undoubtedly exacerbated their mental unfitness for disciplined academic work, but it was not the ultimate cause of this condition. For this it is necessary to look further, and perhaps the most important causes which emerge are housing, child-rearing methods and child labour.

The houses of the poor had always been cold, uncomfortable and insanitary. It is not at all certain that the houses thrown up for factory operatives in the industrial towns were individually worse than the cottages of rural workers. Trouble arose when thousands of these dwellings were jammed together in the smallest possible space and when existing houses were subdivided repeatedly to avoid the expense of purchasing land and because workpeople were unable to travel long distances to work in the period before rapid public transport. In every industrial town huge numbers of back to back houses were built, often, to save space, in hollow squares so that the inner houses faced into a totally enclosed court, reached by a tunnel, and containing the privies which were used by all the houses in the block. The houses consisted of three rooms, one above the other, about eleven feet square, the upper room often given up to some kind of work – framework-knitting or needlework. Nottingham, where there was a particular shortage of building land, was thought to have developed the system of building in courts as far as it would go.

Here they are clustered upon one another, court within court and yard within yard in a manner which defies description ... The courts are, almost without exception, approached through a low arched tunnel, of some 30 to 36 inches wide and 20 to 30 feet long. The courts are noisome, narrow, unprovided with adequate means for the removal of refuse; ill-ventilated and wretched in the extreme, with a gutter, or surface drain, running down the middle. They have no back yards and the privies are common to the whole court; altogether they present scenes of a deplorable character, and of surprising filth and discomfort.

By crowding houses together in this manner it was possible to produce a population density of 500 or more persons to the acre. There was no drainage of any kind, water was provided by water sellers at $\frac{1}{4}d.$ per bucket, or $\frac{1}{2}d.$ per bucket (of three gallons) if the water had to be carried any distance, and the privies were emptied by 'muck majors' who bought the sewage which they stored ready to sell as manure to market gardeners. It is not surprising that such areas were breeding grounds of cholera and similar diseases.

It may be, however, that living conditions were even worse in those towns where it was customary to sub-divide houses which were let by the room. This was very common in towns of historic importance like London and Liverpool where property which had once been respectable had gone down in the world because of the migration of the upper and middle classes to the suburbs. Large houses thus became available for tenements and could provide very profitable investments for the landlords. Engels, in *The Condition of the Working Class in England*, published in 1845, mentions that a room on the first storey commanded the highest rent at 4s. 6d. per week; ground floor and second floor rooms came next at 4s.; followed by garret and cellar dwellings at 3s. per week. He writes about one area in London: 'In the parishes of St John and St Margaret there lived in 1840, according to the Journal of the Statistical Society, 5,366 working men's families in 5,294 'dwellings' (if they deserve the name), men women and children thrown together without distinction of age or sex, 26,830 persons all told, and of these families three fourths possessed but one room.' Of Bethnal Green, he says, 'it is nothing unusual to find a man, his wife, four or five children, and, sometimes, both grandparents, all in one single room where they eat, sleep and work'. He records one Dickensian scene which strikes off the misery and squalor of the inhabitants of such 'dwellings'; it is the record of an inquest held in 1843:

She had lived at No. 3, White Lion Court, Bermondsey, with her husband and a nineteen year old son, in a little room in which neither a bedstead nor any other furniture was to be seen. She lay dead beside her son upon a heap of feathers which were scattered over her almost naked body, there being neither sheet nor coverlet. The feathers stuck so fast over the whole body that the physician could not examine the corpse until it was cleansed and then found it starved and scarred from the bites of vermin. Part of the floor of the room was torn up and the hole used by the family as a privy.

This was an extreme case; death from starvation was not common even in such surroundings, but, according to the report of 1845 on the 'State of Large Towns and Populous Places', there were 20,000 people in Manchester and 45,000 in Liverpool living in cellars. Three-quarters of all the houses in Nottingham were built back to back. Leicester had no piped water supply of any kind for nearly 12,000 houses. And the fact remains that in these towns the mean age at death was below twenty years and fewer than half working-class children survived to five years of age. Engels remarks about the slums of Manchester: 'In a word we must confess that in the working men's dwellings of Manchester, no cleanliness, no convenience, and consequently no comfortable family life is possible; that in such dwellings only a physically degenerate race, robbed of all humanity, degraded, reduced, morally and physically, to bestiality could feel comfortable and at home.' If Engels, because of his association with Marx is regarded as a tainted source, it is possible to refer to the curiously similar remark made, in the same year, by the author of the report on large towns and populous places about the courts of Nottingham: 'In such quarters it is hardly possible that a family can preserve for any term of years, either decency, morals or health.'

An important contributory factor to the high infant death rate was the ignorance and incompetence displayed in child care. Contemporary investigators sometimes attributed this to lack of domestic instruction in schools, but probably the most important reason was that working-class mothers were almost invariably employed in factories, warehouses or in domestic industries so that they had no time either to look after their babies or to give their daughters any kind of domestic training. As one observer remarked: 'Taken to work at the tenderest age, when they marry they are as uneducated for wives and mothers as if they had been brought from the Sandwich Islands and expected to manage an English establishment in Regent Street. To this unhappy condition is referred some of the excessive mortality of infants, and much of the dissolute and reckless habits of the husbands.'

The fact that women returned to their work at the first possible moment after a confinement meant that there was a thriving industry concerned with providing domestic assistance to working mothers – washing, house cleaning, baby minding. The Mayor of Manchester in 1844, estimated that the average working-class family paid 2s. per week to various women for domestic help. This was a sizeable outlay, about equivalent to a week's rent, but when a mother could earn 5s. or 7s. 6d. per week in a factory or by the needle at home it was obviously a good investment. Many women made a living by providing such domestic services, usually specializing in one particular line – as washerwoman, nurse and so on, and, in Nottingham at any rate, there was a fairly standard rate of 2s. per week for which a baby could be cared for while the mother was at work. Women who took in domestic needlework from warehouses frequently employed a young girl of five or six years to act as nurse and to help with the needlework when the child or children were asleep and again a wage of 1s. 6d. to 2s. was usual. According to a coroner 'infant mortality in Nottingham is enormously great and he had no doubt that one of the chief causes was the practice of putting the children out to nurse; in fact it was his conviction that in many cases they were put out because the mothers wanted to get rid altogether of an incumbrance'.

Whether the infants were put out to nurse with professional baby farmers or kept at home while the mother worked, they were frequently dosed with opiates to keep them quiet, the most popular of these being 'Godfrey's Cordial'. This was made of laudanum dissolved in treacle. The standard London form of the cordial contained up to two tea-spoonsful of laudanum to the quart, but in the provinces it was frequently made much stronger. It was the custom to begin the administration of the cordial within a few days of birth and to increase the dose until a dose of two teaspoonsful three times per day was reached when the child was put on to neat laudanum. The increasing dose was dictated not only by the growth of the child but by the fact that laudanum, a derivative of opium, is highly addictive so that larger quantities were continually needed to produce an effect. A chemist in an industrial town in the Midlands described the practice as follows:

The practice is begun in three or four weeks after birth, and continued, if the child should live, till two years, but in the majority of cases the children die before they reach that age. They generally go off as in consumption, 'in a waste'. They become pale and wan with sharpness of features. The mothers come and ask openly for laudanum. They begin with syrup of rhubarb and Godfrey's mixed together; then they go to Godfrey's pure and then to laudanum as the effects become by habit diminished. Half a teaspoonful of equal parts of Godfrey's and rhubarb is the dose to begin with; very soon this is increased to two teaspoonsful; these doses he believes (has no doubt) are given three times a day. When the pure Godfrey's is used about one teaspoonful is given, and they will go on to two teaspoonsful and then they begin with laudanum. This is at first administered in five drops thrice a day, and it is increased to twenty drops; does not think that this is exceeded; 'the child is by this time either off the mother's hands by age, or dead'.

Another chemist gave an example to illustrate the practice:

A case occurred a short time ago of a mother coming into the shop with her child in her arms. Witness remonstrated against giving it laudanum, and told the woman she had better take the child home and put it in a bucket of water – 'it would have been the most humane place of putting it out of the way'. The mother replied that the child had been used to the laudanum and must have it, and that it took a halfpenny worth a day, or 60 drops. Does not know what has become of the child, but 'supposes it is done for by this time'.

The custom of administering opiates to infants was not a minor evil but a very widespread one. The chemist whose evidence has just been quoted testified in 1842 that he sold a gallon of laudanum per week, retail, and that a number of other chemists in the district sold 'many gallons each in the year'. A coroner gave an example of a chemist, in the same town, who made up thirteen hundredweight of treacle into Godfrey's Cordial every year. In her *Household Management*, Mrs Beeton mentioned that hired nurses habitually used Godfrey's, and warned parents of its dangers.

The evidence given by Mary Colton to the Children's Employment Commission of 1842 sums up the conditions under which many working-class mothers attempted to bring up children. It describes the treatment of infants and suggests the reasons for this treatment. Mary Colton was a twenty-year-old woman who took in needlework from a lace warehouse in Nottingham:

Has worked at the lace piece since she was six years old for fourteen or fifteen hours a day on the average; used to commence at 6 a.m. in the summer and left off at 10 at night; in winter at half past 8 a.m. and worked till 10 p.m.; could earn from a shilling to five shillings per week. Was in the habit of sitting from 6 a.m. to 10 p.m. when the work was urgent; never went home for her meals until she was confined; sometimes had half an hour (for meals) oftener not. Was confined of an illegitimate child in November 1839. When the child was a week old she gave it half a teaspoonful of Godfrey's twice a day. She could not afford to pay for the nursing of the child, and so gave it Godfrey's to keep it quiet, that she might not be interrupted at the lace piece; she gradually increased the quantity by the drop or two at a time until it became a teaspoonful; when the infant was four months old it was so 'wankle' and thin that folks persuaded her to give it laudanum to bring it on as it did other children. A halfpenny worth, which was about a teaspoonful and threequarters was given in two days; continued to give her this quantity since February 1840 until this last February past (1841), and then reduced the quantity. She now buys a halfpenny worth of laudanum and a halfpenny worth of Godfrey's mixed, which lasts her three days.

Can earn about three shillings a week now, working from 9 a.m. to 10 p.m., having one hour for dinner and three quarters of an hour for tea. If it had not been for her having to sit so close to her work she would never have given the child Godfrey's. She has tried to break it off many times, but cannot, for if she did, she would not have anything to eat.

A note attached to Mary Colton's evidence by the resident surgeon of the poor law union provides the inevitable conclusion to this pathetic account: 'This infant was brought to me in the last stages of marasmus, suffering under very considerable diarrhoea, and will not, in all probability, live many weeks.'

The account of Mary Colton's life raises the third factor which militated against the readiness of working-class children for education – child labour. In every industry at this time there was a high demand for unskilled labour to perform tasks which would now be performed by machinery; the degree of mechanization achieved by English industry at this stage of the industrial revolution is easily exaggerated. Much of this work was repetitive and required no great amount of skill or strength and was therefore open to children who had the great advantage, from the employers' point of view, that they would accept wages far below an economic level for adults. The kind of work undertaken by children varied, of course, almost infinitely, but one or two examples may help to illustrate the situation. In mines children, boys and girls, were employed underground to control the ventilating doors, sitting for hours at a time, often in total darkness. Children as young as five years were engaged in this work and others, rather older, were used to push tubs of coal or waste along the roads of the mines. In lace-making children, mainly boys, were engaged as winders or threaders. Winders had the job of winding thread on to the bobbins which were used in the machines while threaders had to 'set up' the machines, which involved threading some 1,800 needles with thread from the bobbins. Child labour was by no means confined to the industrial towns or to large-scale industries. There was still a great deal of domestic work, some industries, like hosiery, remaining organized on the smallest scale until well after the middle of the nineteenth century, while some of the worst cases of sweating and ill-treatment came from agricultural gangs, groups of children under a master who took on agricultural labour for farmers on a contract basis and frequently lived a nomadic existence.

It is very difficult to make any useful general statement about the age at which children started work. Perhaps the nearest one can get is to say that it would be the exceptional working-class child who had not begun by eleven years. It seems to have been the custom for children in hosiery, lace and textile areas to start work about the age of seven years in domestic work or in small workshops and to graduate around the age of eleven to the larger concerns whose proprietors were beginning by the 1840s to express concern about the employment of very young children. This was one of many examples of the fact that the worst abuses were generally to be found in small workshops where the margin of profits was very fine and where humanitarian sentiments could not be afforded. Mining companies were notoriously bad employers and children regularly started work in them at five or younger; it was also notorious that acts of Parliament prohibiting the employment of women and children underground were regularly ignored. In agriculture there was not much work, except of a casual nature, for children below ten years of age, although the situation varied very considerably from place to place, presumably according to the type of farming characteristic of the area. Thus children started work later and were considered to be better treated in the East Riding than in Cambridgeshire, while there were black spots even in the East Riding, like the district round Howden and Goole, where a high rate of infant mortality was attributed to the employment of women in field work.

Children could begin work very young indeed especially when their parents were engaged in work which was done at home or in small workshops, and it was repeatedly observed that parents were frequently the worst exploiters of their children's labour. A woman called Mary Thorpe described to the Children's Employment Commission of 1862 the work of children in the domestic hosiery industry in Arnold, then a village a few miles north of Nottingham, where almost the whole population was engaged in framework-knitting and stitching up or 'seaming' the resulting garments. This village specialized at the time in glove-making.

Little children here begin work at stitching gloves when very young. My little sister, now $5\frac{1}{2}$ years old, can stitch a good many little fingers (this girl began at $3\frac{1}{2}$ years). She used to stand on a stool so as to be able to see the candle on the table. I have seen many begin as young as that and they do so still . . . Children younger than seven but not younger than six are kept up as late as that (i.e. 11 or 12 p.m. on a Friday). Mothers will pin them to their knee to keep them to their work, and, if they are sleepy, give them a slap on the side of the head to keep them awake . . . little girls of eight or so go out to nurse a baby, and have to stitch while the baby is asleep during the day, and they are kept to stitch after the baby is put to bed.

Hours of work and rates of pay also varied enormously and only a few general remarks can be made about them. Twelve hours per day was nothing out of the ordinary and longer hours were common. Children often did not object to overtime because it was customary for them to keep overtime pay for themselves, their ordinary wage going to their parents, except for perhaps a penny per week pocket money. All industries experienced violent fluctuations in their activity, due to seasonal variations or to market demand and when a business was working at full pressure, sixteen, eighteen or twenty-four hours at a stretch was usual. A particular reason for fluctuation of hours in the domestic industries was the workers' habit of taking Monday and often Tuesday as a holiday in addition to the weekend, and then working from Friday morning straight through to Saturday night to catch up. Many observers noted the effect of this upon the very young children who were employed as ancillaries to these trades.

The amount of active ill-treatment received by children also varied with the trade. Some of the work which children were expected to do was far beyond them physically and inevitably led to deformity or sickness. Engels records of the nail-makers of the Black Country that:

Girls and boys work from the tenth or twelfth year, and are accounted fully skilled only when they make 1,000 nails a day. For 1,200 nails the pay is $5\frac{3}{4}d$. Every nail receives twelve blows and since the hammer weighs $1\frac{1}{4}$ lb, the nailer must lift 18,000 lb to earn this miserable pay. With this hard work and insufficient food the children inevitably develop ill-formed, under-sized frames ... They know nothing of any different kind of life than that in which they toil from morning until they are allowed to stop at night, and did not even understand the question, never heard before, whether they were tired.

Work in the silk mills in Macclesfield, the cotton mills of the Manchester area and the West Riding woollen mills produced extensive deformities in children, often amounting to disablement.

Malformations of the spine are very frequent among mill-hands; some of them consequent upon mere overwork, others the effect of long work upon constitutions originally feeble or weakened by bad food. Deformities seem even more frequent than these diseases; the knees were bent inward, the ligaments very often relaxed and enfeebled, and the long bones of the legs bent. The thick end of these long bones were especially apt to be bent and disproportionately developed

The Macclesfield silk mills were considered the worst, because of the very early age, five to six years, at which children commenced work; one witness records having counted sixty-three serious cripples in the streets of the town.

Other trades were obviously unhealthy, sometimes dangerously so. The pottery industry included several of these:

By far the most injurious is the work of those who dip the finished article into a fluid containing great quantities of lead, and often of arsenic, or have to take the freshly-dipped article up with the hands. The hands and clothing of these workers, adults and children, are always wet with this fluid, the skin softens and falls off through constant contact with rough objects, so that the fingers often bleed, and are constantly in a state most favourable for the absorption of this dangerous substance. The consequence is violent pain, and serious disease of the stomach and intestines, obstinate constipation, colic, sometimes consumption, and, most common of all, epilepsy among children ... One witness relates that two children who worked with him died of convulsions at their work; another who had helped with the dipping two years while a boy, relates that he had violent pains in the bowels at first, then convulsions, in consequence of which he was confined to his bed two months, since when the attacks of convulsions have increased in frequency, are now daily, accompanied often by ten to twenty epileptic fits, his right arm is paralysed ... In one factory were found in the dipping house four men, all epileptic and afflicted with severe colic, and eleven boys, several of them already epileptic.

In many trades conditions were less extravagantly dangerous and unhealthy. The work in hosiery and lace, for example, was not especially heavy and there does not appear to have been very much systematic ill-treatment of children. Some of the large employers were notably enlightened for the period and one encounters kindness in some unexpected quarters. There is an account in the 1862 Children's Employment Commission of a small workshop in one of the squalid courts for which Nottingham was notorious: 'the yard is sixteen feet wide and eight or ten houses deep, with what appears to be a privy and ash-pit common to all the houses at the further end, and a pump in the middle, with a gutter containing some stagnant water and refuse running from it'. This workshop was one of the most crowded of all those investigated by the commission, but the treatment of the young children who worked there was surprising:

Much care and kindness seem to be bestowed upon the children by the mistress and her daughter who overlook them. One, a girl of eight, who knew only some of her letters and no figures, repeated to me almost without mistake two very long ballad-hymns about little children which she had been taught at work by her mistress ... Mrs Newton, the over-looker in the top room gives them 'drops' or something as rewards to encourage them, and if they get many in a week, adds something, perhaps three-halfpence, as overtime to their wages, so many 'drops' counting a halfpenny. Gives each child a halfpenny for herself in addition to her wages ... often lets the children have books from the library.

Nevertheless, although individual employers might prove kind, the fact remains that the children of the poor started work, at the latest by ten or eleven years of age, usually much earlier. They worked upwards of twelve hours per day for a few shillings a week, which was taken by the parents who left them perhaps a penny. The jobs they took were unskilled and repetitive, offering no training or hope of advancement. From the 1830s onwards acts of Parliament were passed which effected some amelioration of conditions in certain industries, particularly in those which were organized in large units. These, however, were of limited effect. They were difficult to apply without a larger administrative establishment than any nineteenth-century British government was prepared to countenance, and many industries were still partly or wholly organized on the basis of small workshops and private houses which evaded factory legislation.

Under these circumstances it is not surprising that the attitude of the working class towards their conditions of life varied from misery and hopelessness to a bitterness which frequently broke out into rioting and smashing of the machinery to which they attributed some of their troubles. Half of the working class in 1867 were estimated to live upon an income of 10–12s. per week, which meant that they were perpetually upon the edge of starvation, and, in the frequent depressions they were dependent upon the uncertainties of public charity or the rigours of the poor law. The extra income which wife and children could earn was critical to such families and it was this factor above all which kept such children out of school. The school fees, perhaps 2d. or 3d. per week were not in themselves a great outlay except in large families, but only parents who were very determined to provide their children with an education would forego the 2s. 6d. or 3s. 6d. per week which a child of seven or eight could easily earn when business was good.

Life in the slums of an industrial town was not only dangerous; as Engels and others pointed out it was also demoralizing for the survivors. The squalid, insanitary houses and filthy atmosphere turned housekeeping into a heart-breaking task even for the mother who was not already employed in a more than full time job. Towns of all sizes were by modern standards remarkably deficient in any facilities for recreation. The members of the upper working class were very active in producing institutions of their own both for recreation and for self-improvement. They formed friendly societies, libraries, debating societies and similar clubs and institutions of all kinds. These were almost invariably held in public houses for want of any alternative accommodation and had a convivial side which drew an undue amount of censure from middle-class observers who always took a puritanical view of working-class entertainments. These societies were also regarded with suspicion because their political affiliations were often of a radical nature. The bulk of the working classes, however, were not attracted to these societies which were patronized by respectable, articulate men with a measure of education. Their pleasures were rougher and it is not surprising that in their very limited leisure time they were inclined to try to forget their miseries in drink, while drug-taking was a very general practice.

A large quantity of solid opium is also sold; it is common in many of the shops to keep it ready prepared in small packets, like other articles in constant demand; these are sold at a penny or twopence each ... The solid opium is consumed exclusively by adults, men and women, but more by the latter than the former, in the proportion of three to one ... It is common practice among a large portion of the poorest class of mechanics, inhabiting such places as 'the Becks' and 'Meadow Platts', habitually to use opium in the fluid or solid form. Has some customers who take as much as an ounce of opium a day; knows one woman who has taken that quantity in his shop.

A particular grievance of the working class was the introduction under the factory system of new working habits. Under the domestic system the speed at which a man worked was to a great extent his own business. He would generally have a quantity of work to produce by a given time, very often Saturday evening being the deadline, but he enjoyed considerable freedom in spacing his work during the week, and, as was mentioned earlier, it was the very general custom for domestic workers to take a long weekend which included Monday and sometimes even part of Tuesday. This was hard on the children employed in the ancillary trades from one point of view, because of the long hours worked at the end of the week, but, on the other hand, all workers enjoyed some free time on Sundays and Mondays while work proceeded at a relatively leisurely pace on Tuesdays and Wednesdays.

All this was changed with the introduction of factories and large workshops. To the factory owners time wasted was money wasted and in a large concern serious dislocation could be caused by the casual and haphazard time-keeping of the worker accustomed to the domestic system. They therefore insisted upon punctuality and regular attendance and overseers concentrated upon keeping the work going without interruption throughout the day. On this issue the values of employer and workmen were directly opposed and a positive crusade was conducted to instil 'habits of industry' into the working class, the elementary school being regarded as an important agency on the side of the employers. It is not necessary to suppose that the employers' attack upon the working habits of the poor was motivated by malice; in the factory work had to proceed at a steady pace and there was no room for the violent fluctuations in speed characteristic of the domestic worker's week. But we can see that the unmitigated tedium of work in the factories must have been intensely depressing for adults, while for children the lack of any time or opportunity for recreation or change of activity was perhaps as damaging as the actual physical pressure of work.

It was against this background that the elementary school teachers did their work. From our point of view the important feature was the sheer immensity of their task which meant that the efforts of the voluntary agencies were bound to fail even with substantial government financial aid. Indeed the great lesson of this period, in education as in related fields of social welfare was that only massive government intervention could effect real improvement.

CHAPTER 4

THE CHANGING SCHOOL: ADMINISTRATIVE
AND ORGANIZATIONAL CHANGES, 1800-1939

From an administrative point of view the development of popular education in England may be seen as falling into three divisions. The first, from about 1780 to 1870 was the period when all elementary schools were provided and maintained by voluntary effort, assisted after 1833 by a progressively increasing amount of government grant. In the second, from 1870 to 1903, school attendance was made compulsory, and elected school boards had the power to levy rates for the support of schools, while both board and voluntary schools continued to be subsidized from government sources. In 1902 education was brought within the orbit of the normal local government and has continued to be administered by a partnership of the central government with local education authorities. The whole period reflects a growing degree of state intervention in education, and one question to be considered in this chapter is why this occurred. Along with this development went a demand for an ever higher standard of work, and it will be necessary to discuss why this was so, and what were its consequences.

At the end of the eighteenth century it was possible for a parent to obtain a good schooling for his children if he was prepared to pay for it, since there was a variety of private schools, ranging from expensive residential academies which prepared the children of the well-to-do for university, to dame schools which aimed to do no more than look after a few babies while their mothers were at work. As might be expected, the efficiency of private schools varied in general with the fee they charged. A sound education could be had in a day school for 2s. or 3s. per week, which would fit a boy for a respectable job in an office or counting house, and this was within the reach of a skilled artisan, who would expect to pay about the same amount or a little more in rent. Schools which charged 9d. or less per week were regarded as being available to the poor, and the curriculum in these was normally confined to the three 'R's, the cheapest schools being content with teaching reading. Apart from private schools there were charity schools in most towns and many villages, the majority of these having been founded in the early eighteenth century under the auspices of the Society for Promoting Christian Knowledge. But at this period these schools were generally in a state of decline, and were rarely very large, most charities being limited to the education of a limited number of poor pupils.

Thus, when it was proposed to undertake the education of the poor in general in the 1780s it was necessary to start from scratch, and the first attempt at providing universal elementary education was the Sunday School movement. The beginning of the movement is generally attributed to Robert Raikes, a newspaper proprietor of Gloucester, and although isolated earlier ventures have been discovered it is certain that the great development of Sunday schools followed the publicity which he gave to the idea in the 1780s.

In view of the fact that children began work at an exceedingly early age it was a sensible notion to use the one day when they were not employed to provide them with education, and the plan had the added advantage that on Sundays there was a plentiful supply of amateurs to assist with the teaching. It was the use of amateur teachers, which became general after the early years of the movement, which allowed Sunday schools to attain a pupil-teacher ratio immensely better than any other nineteenth-century educational institution; in 1851 the number of pupils per teacher in Sunday schools varied from an average of 5·2 in Methodist schools to 12·3 in Anglican schools. At the same date 80 pupils per teacher was the usual thing in day schools and a much higher figure was not uncommon. The advantage enjoyed by Sunday schools in this respect is too obvious to require comment, but it is worthwhile to observe that there was a reverse side to the employment of amateur teachers. It was pointed out in 1842 by one of the officials who carried out enquiries for the Children's Employment Commission that, for all their zeal, they were frequently incompetent:

The Sunday school teachers, who have by their unpaid and most meritorious services conferred the deepest benefits on the community, must yet as a body be regarded as not duly qualified for the highly important office they have undertaken. They have not generally paid any attention to the subject of education as a thing requiring in itself to be studied by all who aspire to the art of communicating knowledge to others; they are selected from the congregation rather on the grounds of moral and religious conduct than of any peculiar fitness for the office of teacher.

In addition it may well be that the vast number of amateurs engaged in Sunday schools – 318,000 in 1851 – helped to keep the teaching profession in its chronically depressed state throughout the nineteenth century.

As an instrument of secular instruction Sunday schools achieved disappointing results considering the time, effort and money spent upon them. The hours of attendance were inadequate, the curriculum was almost invariably confined to reading and religious instruction, and the teaching was frequently inefficient. By the early years of the nineteenth century their failure to solve the social and political problems which had inspired their establishment was evident. An attempt was made to improve their efficiency by the formation of Sunday School Unions which co-ordinated their efforts, sustained enthusiasm and sometimes published books, but at the same time attention turned towards the provision of day schools. The simultaneous advocacy of the 'mutual' or 'monitorial' system by Bell and Lancaster encouraged this proposal since it was promised that the system would provide cheap education for a large number of pupils – 500 or more to one teacher according to Lancaster.[1] The history of education from the establishment of monitorial schools until the 1870 Act may be viewed as the progressive realization by all interested parties of the size and complexity of the problem of providing universal elementary education.

In this period elementary schools faced two major problems, finance, and the short and irregular school life of the pupils. It was the repeated efforts to solve these which led to the developments to be considered in the following section.

Finance was the constant pre-occupation of school managers and the problem possessed two aspects. In large towns or where substantial private benefactors could be found, it was not particularly difficult to establish schools, and, in favourable circumstances, even to provide a new building. But in impoverished areas, and especially in newly populated districts, where the parochial organization was either nonexistent or swamped by expansion, it was often not possible to raise the funds necessary to start a school. The building grants instituted by the government in 1833 did not solve this problem since any grant made was dependent upon the raising of local funds, a circumstance which caused some contemporary authorities to argue that the effect of the grants was to cause schools to be built where they were least needed. For most managers, however, troubles only began when the school was founded, since it was the almost universal experience that subscriptions fell away sharply once the first enthusiasm for a school had died away. It was a

---

[1] The monitorial system is discussed in chapter 5, below.

prosperous school which had an income of £100 per year, and a teacher of any quality would expect a minimum of £60 as salary. Thus when rent, heating and lighting had been paid for, there was very little for equipment and stationery – or for prizes for conduct and attendance. Most schools had to manage on far less than this, budgets of £40 to £50 were common, and this meant that it was impossible to employ a teacher who was efficient even by the standards of the day, while such schools were constantly running into debt. It was calculated in 1845 that the average national school over-spent its budget by £7 per year; on an income of £50–£100 such a debt would soon mount to a crippling burden.

It was the financial problem which dictated the organization of the elementary schools of the period. It was out of the question for a school to pay for more than one adult teacher. The great majority of schools had only one teacher who taught all children of all ages, or under the monitorial system, supervised their teaching by monitors. Very large town schools were divided into boys', girls' and infants' departments with teachers in charge of each. The master of the boys' department was usually the headmaster, while the infant teacher was paid at a lower rate than the girls' mistress. Adult assistant teachers were virtually unknown; out of 467 schools which had certificated teachers in the Midland area in 1855, only three had adult assistants. School architecture reflected school organization. Schools of the period were invariably built with one large schoolroom in which the teacher operated, while there were one or two small 'classrooms' in which monitors or pupil teachers could work with small groups of children. The plan depended on there being one teacher responsible for the whole school with only semi-trained, semi-adult assistance. Many such buildings are still in use and present a problem where three or four adult teachers have to teach simultaneously.

It was the financial problem, too, which drew the state into the field of elementary education in spite of the ingrained opposition of nineteenth-century thinkers to such intervention. The first tentative step came in 1833 with the grant of £20,000 for the building of school houses. The sum was small but it was of great importance as a precedent and its significance was increased by its context. It must be considered along with the factory act of the same year, and with the grant of public money to recompense the owners of slaves freed by the abolition of slavery within the Empire in 1834. Together, these measures constituted a major breach in the principle of laissez-faire. The factory act broke important new ground by stipulating for the appointment of inspectors to supervise the application of its measures, a precedent very soon to be followed in education, while both the abolition of slavery and the Treasury grant to schools established the principle that the government was prepared to spend public money in redressing social grievances.

From the first building grant the spread of government influence in elementary education was very rapid. The Committee of Privy Council for Education was established in 1839, providing for the first time a government department with specific responsibility for education, and owing to the energy of its first secretary, Sir James Kay-Shuttleworth, it was soon adopting a very positive approach to educational policy making. In 1846 the pupil-teacher system was set up, and the principle established that government grants could be made for the maintenance as well as the building of schools. By this time inspectors of schools existed, and by insisting on the achievement of certain standards before payment of maintenance grant, the government was directly influencing the development of elementary education.

Even where schools could be provided and adequately maintained it proved to be impossible to persuade parents to send children to school regularly enough and for long enough to secure for them an efficient education, even by the undemanding standards of the time. No figures exist for the early years of the century, but in the 1840s inspectors and other investigators were agreed that working-class children attended school on the average for between one and two years, frequently interrupted by periods of unemployment, and that very few remained after ten years of age. The figures do not allow of any great accuracy upon this point, but it seems that one-third, or rather more, of children did not attend day school at all at this period. There was some small improvement in this situation in the middle of the century so far as attracting children into school was concerned. The building grants encouraged a rapid increase in the number of public elementary schools at this time. There was also a small but significant increase in the length of school life. In 1852 53 per cent of pupils in inspected schools had been in attendance for less than one year, and 73 per cent for less than two years; by 1861 the proportions were 38 per cent and 61 per cent.[1] But there was no similar improvement in the age of pupils; at both dates rather over 50 per cent of pupils were under eight years and less than 15 per cent over eleven years, and the latter group consisted very largely of pupil-teachers. It should be remembered, too, that these figures related only to inspected schools which were, on the whole, the most efficient. If all elementary schools, private and public, had been taken into account the situation would have been found to be worse still. In the 1860s it

[1] *Minutes of Committee of Privy Council on Education* (1852/3), App. I, Table I; (1864/5), App. I, Table I.

remained true that a very substantial proportion of working-class children never went to day school, and that those who did so, attended irregularly and for a grossly inadequate period.

For a variety of reasons the question of public provision of elementary education came to a head in the 1860s, and among much discussion the country moved decisively towards a substantial measure of state control. Finance was, as might be expected, one of the most important factors in this development. The cost of the exchequer grants to schools had risen dramatically since 1833:

1833	£20,000
1851	£150,000
1857	£541,000
1859	£837,000

It will be observed that the rise had been particularly sharp in the 1850s, and it was not unreasonable for people to ask whether the money was being wisely spent, especially since the country had just experienced an expensive war, in which the efficiency both of the army and of government departments had come under sharp questioning. Certain periods in the history of education may be characterized by phrases which were in use at the time. In 1944 much was heard of 'equality of opportunity'; in the 1860s it was 'a *sound* and *cheap* elementary education'.

At the same time there was a new realization that the problem was not merely one of school provision but of bringing children into school. One of the most prominent features of the evidence produced by the Newcastle Commission which reported in 1861 was the number of children who did not go to school and of the irregularity of the attendance of those who did go. But the Newcastle Commission only added material to an existing body of evidence concerning the size and complexity of the educational problem. A succession of enquiries into children's employment, notably those of 1842, 1844 and 1862, demonstrated how rare was an efficient education among working-class children, and the educational census of 1851 provided the first reliable statistics upon which to base discussions of educational problems. The relation between ignorance and other social problems was emphasized by investigations such as the Commission of Enquiry into the State of Large Towns and Populous Places, of 1845. Public interest in elementary education was reflected in Parliament by a succession of abortive education bills which were intended to systematize and expand the haphazard provision of elementary schooling. Outside Parliament numerous associations were formed to forward the cause of public education. These associations fell into different, and frequently embattled, groups according to whether they favoured on the one hand state intervention or private enterprise, and on the other whether they were secular or religious in tone. The main fact which emerges from their bitter controversies was that public opinion was sharply divided on both issues, and that no government could hope for general approval for any decision which it might make.

The dispute between these associations introduces the religious question which had haunted elementary education since the days of Bell and Lancaster. From the earliest days the movement to establish monitorial schools had divided into two camps which may be described with a fair degree of accuracy as representing the Anglican and Nonconformist interests respectively. The 'National School Society' was founded by the Church and the Dissenters set up the 'British and Foreign School Society'. Relations between the two interests worsened, at a national level at least, and successive education bills were torpedoed by the opposition of one side or the other.

The ferocity of the sectarian warfare was undoubtedly a barrier to progress, and there is evidence to suggest that the hostility was sustained by enthusiastic controversialists when most people were, in their cooler moments, willing to seek an accommodation. But there were genuine problems. About three quarters of all elementary schools were founded and run by the Church of England, which had something like a monopoly in rural areas. In villages it would often have been quite uneconomical to establish a separate school for Dissenters, while there is no doubt that some Church schools in such areas indulged in proselytizing which bitterly offended Dissenting parents. From the 1830s onwards there was a progressive tendency for the Dissenters to turn away from the provision of their own schools and to favour a state system. They also frequently proposed that instruction in schools should be secular, religious instruction being provided by ministers of different denominations, perhaps at some time in the school timetable set aside for the purpose. The Church, in contrast, continued to advocate the provision of its own schools, and some of its most vigorous efforts in this direction were made after the establishment of school boards.

From the administrative point of view there was need for reform since the existing method of distributing the government grant was hopelessly complicated and unwieldy. By 1860 there were several thousand schools and departments in receipt of grant, and the Education Department, which had succeeded the Committee of Privy Council in 1856 corresponded separately with each of these. In addition all certificated teachers who were training pupil-teachers, and the pupil-teachers themselves received separate payments from the Department. The system was obviously over-centralized, but there was a great obstacle in the way of any devolution of power. This was the absence of any system of local government. Outside the municipal boroughs there were, until the appearance of county councils in 1889, only poor law unions and ecclesiastical parishes. The unions were intensely unpopular among working people while attempts to relate educational administration to the parish invariably foundered upon the opposition of Dissenters who, not altogether unreasonably, were suspicious of the power which such an organization would place in the hands of the established Church. The problem of educational administration was to be a recurrent one. In 1870 it was solved for the moment by the establishment of school boards, local authorities with specific responsibility for elementary education. These, however, were still too numerous and often too small for efficiency, while they encountered bitter opposition from county councils and the corporations of boroughs, which wished to assume power over education. In 1902 education was brought within the compass of normal local government, which involved a massive reduction in the number of education authorities. The number was reduced again in 1944 by the elimination of what were called 'Part Three Authorities', and in 1974 another major re-organization made a further reduction, many smaller authorities disappearing. On each occasion the motive of administrative neatness has been important, but there has also been the hope that larger education authorities would provide a more even distribution of educational facilities.

The first attempt to solve the complex problem of public elementary education was described by its author, Robert Lowe, with much accuracy as a reversion to the principle of free trade. The essence of 'payment by results', as the scheme introduced by the Revised Code of 1862 was always called, was that payment of government grant to a school depended upon two factors. A basic grant was paid for any child who attended a fixed number of times in a year. Further grants were paid for any children, qualified by attendance, who passed examinations in any of the three 'R's. Pupils were tested in a higher 'standard' each year, a narrowly defined syllabus being laid down by the Education Department for each standard. Subsequently regulations were added which allowed supplementary grants to be paid if senior pupils were taught various subjects, referred to as 'class' or 'specific' subjects, according to the way the teaching was organized; but such 'advanced' work was considered definitely subordinate to the school's main work of teaching the rudiments.

The Revised Code was a deliberate negation of the idea of a national system of education. The introduction of compulsion as a solution to the problem of irregular attendance was rejected in favour of a bounty scheme, and the semi-official status of the certificated teacher was undermined when the pension scheme and the payment of supplements to salaries, introduced in the Kay-Shuttleworth era, were abandoned. The emphasis of payment by results was upon finding the cheapest possible way in which the barest rudiments of instruction could be passed on to the children of the working class.

Few educational measures have been so comprehensively damned both by contemporaries and by later historians as the Revised Code, and it is difficult to find any grounds for dissenting from the general opinion. It is probable that there was some improvement in regularity of attendance, often secured at the expense of bringing to school children who were manifestly unfit, and not infrequently in an infectious condition. It has been claimed that there was some improvement in the teaching of the three 'R's, and this may be true. When these points have been made everything has been said which can be said in favour of payment by results. On the other hand nothing whatever was done about bringing non-attenders into school; the system simply ignored the problem. Concentration upon the three 'R's was obtained at the expense of narrowing the elementary school curriculum so that even the tentative experiments in advanced work which had appeared since 1846 were abandoned, while the examination system was based upon a confusion of information with education which rendered the results almost meaningless. The social side of a school's work received no recognition under the code, a curiously illogical omission considering the contemporary importance attached to the socializing role of the school. The status of the teacher, which had been rising steadily was undermined and the teacher and inspector were forced into bitter and long-lasting hostility. The emphasis on routine in a teacher's work was a barrier to progress when a more liberal concept of elementary education was adopted, especially after 1902. The effects of a generation of rigid application of the code were not easily shrugged off.

But if the immediate results of the Revised Code were almost universally disastrous there were certain indirect results which were less unhappy. The public outcry against payment by results, in which virtually every contemporary educationalist joined, gave much publicity to the problem of public elementary education, and the reduction in grant which immediately followed its application worsened the financial position of many schools especially those in impoverished areas, thus underlining the need for positive action. At the same time the total failure of payment by results to achieve either efficiency or cheapness discredited the negative approach. From the financial point of view the reduction in grant was very temporary and the cost to the taxpayer was soon rising again. Attendance remained extremely irregular – 70 per cent was a creditable figure – while no impression whatever was made upon the large proportion of children who never attended school. So far as the level of work was concerned, as late as 1873 only 15 per cent of pupils passed the annual examination in the standard corresponding to their age; 57 per cent were one year too old and 26 per cent were two years too old. The Revised Code established value for money as the criterion for measuring the educational system, and it stood condemned under its own terms. It may well be that public opinion was prepared for a substantial measure of state intervention in 1870 by the demonstration by the Revised Code of the complete inability of private enterprise to solve the problem.

Under the terms of the Elementary Education Act of 1870 and subsequent acts of 1876 and 1880 elementary education was administered by school boards, or, where no board was established, by school attendance committees. The establishment of school boards solved several problems. The financial burden upon school managers was lightened, since boards could issue precepts upon the rates for support of their schools. Schools, therefore, were built and equipped upon more generous lines, more teachers were employed and they were better paid, and the scope of elementary education was widened, the larger boards experimenting, for example, with secondary education and the teaching of handicapped children. The problem of attendance was solved. Most boards adopted by-laws enforcing attendance, and this was made nationally compulsory in 1876. The attendance officers, always popularly known as 'school board men', faced a huge task in large towns, but by the 1890s mass truancy had been overcome and attendance figures were comparable with those of the present day.

An important by-product of compulsory attendance was that the exploitation of child labour was prevented. Successive factory acts failed to do this, partly because of the difficulty of enforcing the acts, partly because much of the worst exploitation, in private houses and small shops and warehouses, fell outside their scope. The school board men, by enforcing the attendance of children at school, prevented their employment elsewhere. This result was not achieved rapidly. Until well into this century local education authorities had to conduct a vigorous campaign, which has not altogether finished today, against the part-time employment of children out of school hours, but there was nothing like the mass exploitation of child labour which had been such a feature of industry in the first two-thirds of the nineteenth century.

Until 1870 it was impossible to draw any clear dividing line between urban and rural schools in respect of size, staffing and equipment. Urban schools did tend to be larger, but the range from large to small schools was not great, a school of 250–300 pupils was unusual even in towns. All schools were equally ill-equipped and very few indeed had more than one teacher. There were great variations in teachers' pay, but it was not necessarily the case that the masters of big urban schools were paid most; such schools were often more poverty stricken than village schools which enjoyed the patronage of a wealthy landowner. But after 1870 a difference appeared between the large and small boards, and the gap between their scale of provision progressively widened. The reason for this was almost entirely financial. The large urban boards could afford to build big schools, to equip and staff them on a relatively luxurious scale, and to attract the most energetic and ambitious teachers by paying high salaries. By contrast the many hundreds of one-school boards still had little financial margin, especially since the members of the boards, certainly the most influential ones, were very likely to be the main ratepayers of the district. It was at this time, therefore, that the great discrepancy appeared between the educational provision of urban and rural areas, which was one of the motives for both the 1902 and 1944 Acts.

In the urban boards large schools were built and this involved the acceptance of a new form of school organization. It was impossible for all the pupils in such schools to be taught by one teacher, particularly since children were staying at school longer so that there was a wider range of ability and age to take account of. At the same time the supply of qualified teachers was improving, and the better financial position of school boards made the appointment of assistant teachers feasible. Thus these schools came to be organized on a class basis, with the pupils divided according to the standard in which they were to sit the annual examination, with an assistant teacher in charge of each standard or group of standards. This reorganization was reflected in the architecture of new schools which were divided into classrooms, a practice which has only very recently been altered even in primary schools. The new system required that assistant teachers be allowed a large degree of autonomy if it was to work efficiently, but it was long before the logic of the situation was appreciated, and head teachers in elementary schools and their successors, primary and secondary modern schools, have often continued to exercise a close and cramping supervision of their assistants, treating them, in effect, as pupil teachers.

In 1902 education passed under the control of local education authorities so that the administrative picture was very much as it is today. It is not clear what the effect of this change was upon those areas which had been administered by one of the big school boards; some of the new education committees were less active and adventurous than their predecessors. But it is quite certain that in rural areas the change was for the better and at least a beginning was made in the process of 'levelling-up' the provision in these districts, although this is by no means complete at the present time.

The most significant result of the Act of 1902 and the events leading to it, however, was the emergence of the government as a major policy-making body in education. In the school board period every advance in educational provision or practice was initiated by individual boards, often in the face of opposition from the Education Department. After 1902 the government was active, either through the Board of Education or more directly through legislation in laying down lines of development for elementary and secondary education.

The effect of government intervention appeared in two directions, a liberalizing of the outlook of the elementary school, and the movement of schools into the field of welfare. In the *Handbook of Suggestions for Teachers*, which was first issued by the Board of Education in 1905, there was a very different spirit at work from that of the old Elementary School Code. The preface indicated a desire for experiment and innovation among teachers:

The only uniformity of practice which the Board of Education desires to see in Public Elementary Schools is that each teacher shall think for himself, and work out for himself such methods of teaching as may use his powers to the best advantage and be best suited to the particular needs and conditions of the school. Uniformity in details of practice (except in the mere routine of school management) is not desirable even if it were attainable.

This attitude was a great advance upon the specific regulations concerning syllabuses and teaching methods which had been imposed upon elementary schools under the Education Department. It is not to be supposed that all schools immediately entered an era of sweetness and light. The tradition of payment by results was too deeply entrenched to be removed quickly; many schools continued to be organized in standards until the Second World War. But a licence was given for enterprising teachers to experiment. In fact some teachers had already been doing so, chiefly in schools administered by the large school boards, some of which had shown a typically nineteenth-century independence in their relations with the Education Department.

At first sight it seems curious that the Board of Education should adopt such an enlightened view of elementary education, since at exactly the same period it was following a distinctly reactionary policy in secondary education, putting an end to higher grade schools, crippling the higher elementary schools with rigid restrictions upon the age of pupils and the syllabus, and insisting, as a condition of payment of grant, that grammar schools should follow a literary, non-vocational curriculum. The paradox, however, is not so extreme as it appears. The higher grade schools were regarded with hostility by Sir Robert Morant and people who shared his views, not on the grounds of inefficiency, but rather because they blurred the division between the elementary and secondary school systems. To such people there was a sharp distinction between these systems which was at least as much social as academic in nature. G. A. N. Lowndes, in *The Silent Social Revolution*, makes this point when he compares the educational provision of the country at that time to the railways, which provided first, second and third class compartments. The public schools comprised the first class, grammar schools and private schools comprised the second class, while elementary schools made up the third class. Each class of school served a different social class and prepared its pupils for different occupational levels.

There is one important qualification to record. Morant had no objection to children transferring from the elementary school to the secondary school; in fact he favoured the process and the 1907 'free place' regulations, which made the first large-scale provision for transfer, were instituted while he was in control at the Board of Education. But he took the same view of transfer as the army took of commissioning a man from the ranks. That is to say that a working-class child who entered a grammar school was expected to take on the ethos of the middle-class institution; he became, *ex officio*, a member of the middle class.

Holding these views, Morant would naturally oppose any scheme which confused the secondary system, which trained 'officers' with the elementary system, which trained 'other ranks'. But this did not mean that he could not campaign for the improvement of the education provided by elementary schools. It was manifestly desirable that the training of 'other ranks' should be efficient even if it was unlike that provided for 'officers', and therefore, so long as the elementary schools kept to their own sphere and did not attempt to rival the secondary school they could expect Morant's support. Thus it was quite logical that Morant should adopt a benevolent attitude towards the liberalization of the elementary school while taking a leading part in the destruction of the higher grade schools.

The change in the Board of Education's attitude towards the elementary school was an administrative matter. No legislation was involved. It was a question of the board adopting an encouraging view of experiment and innovation, and persuading local education authorities to do the same. The chief interest in this development, for the historian, is that, for the first time since the days of Kay-Shuttleworth in the 1840s the government was taking the initiative in educational matters. At the same time, however, legislation was passed which had the effect of greatly increasing the responsibility both of the central and local government for the welfare of children, in and out of school. The initiative taken by the government in educational innovation in the years from 1902 to 1914 was never surrendered, and constitutes one of the major differences between educational administration in the nineteenth and twentieth centuries.

In 1901 the minimum age at which children could be taken into full-time employment was fixed at twelve years, and by acts of 1903 and 1904 local education authorities were empowered to stipulate the age at which children could begin part-time work and the hours within which they could be employed. The bulk of the legislation of this period, however, followed the general election of 1906 when the Liberals were returned with a large majority. This election may be taken as marking the end of the period of nineteenth-century individualism and the beginning of the period of collectivism, and the novelty of the political scene was underlined by the election to the new Parliament of forty Labour members. Driven chiefly by Lloyd George the Liberal government followed an active policy of social reform and the educational measures were only part of a programme which included the beginnings of national insurance and old-age pensions and fiscal measures aimed at breaking up large estates.

In 1906 an act allowed local education authorities to levy a halfpenny rate to subsidize the provision of school dinners for poor children. Some school boards had provided 'penny dinners' at least as early as the 1880s. In Nottingham children received soup and a pudding for a penny, or were sometimes fed with dishes cooked by pupils at the board cookery centres. Other schools provided only bread and dripping with cocoa or coffee. But all these efforts, like the even earlier ventures by 'ragged schools' were financed by voluntary contributions and were necessarily on a rather small scale. After 1906 the provision of school meals could be put on an official basis, although it was not until the Second World War that children came to stay for school dinner as a matter of course.

A number of important measures were introduced in 1907. The 'King's Scholarship' was abolished and the 'bursar' system introduced by which intending elementary school teachers were sent to secondary schools on a scholarship before proceeding to college. This was the beginning of the end of the pupil-teacher system, although this continued with ever diminishing numbers until after the Second World War. The new scheme reduced the severe strain to which pupil-teachers had been subject, and also allowed them to mix with pupils of their own age, whereas, under the pupil-teacher system they had often led an isolated existence, stranded between the pupils in their school who were younger than themselves and the teachers who were much older. At the same time the 'free place' regulations introduced a regular system of transfer from the elementary school to the secondary school. Many schools already offered free places; 23,000 such places were available in 1906, but the new regulations greatly enlarged the provision. By 1913 there were 60,000 free places and by 1927, 143,000. The 'free place' regulations initiated the 'educational ladder' by which working-class children could climb from elementary school to secondary school and eventually to higher education. The problems in the path of the working-class child were not all removed at once. Many parents were unable to take advantage of the secondary school places offered to their children and a depressingly high proportion of children left secondary school at the first opportunity, but the regulations of 1907 remain an important step towards opening secondary and higher education to at least selected members of the working class.

In the same year there were two other important developments. The Probation of Offenders Act was the beginning of a movement towards making the treatment of juvenile offenders separate from that of adults, since the age of the accused person was a factor which the magistrate could take into consideration when deciding whether to make a probation order. In 1908 another important act introduced juvenile courts, thus emphasizing the distinction between the adult and juvenile penal systems. Remand homes were also instituted and experiments were made in the use of reformatory and industrial schools as a means of re-educating the juvenile delinquents. Of more general application was the establishment of the school medical service. Medical inspection of children in elementary schools was made compulsory,[1] and the medical service began a long struggle against infectious and contagious diseases, infestation by vermin and uncleanliness. Apart from the obvious benefits provided by the diagnosis and treatment of disease, the reports of school medical officers were significant in drawing attention to the physical conditions which afflicted so many children. Public concern had already

---

[1] Treatment was not compulsory until 1921.

been aroused on this topic by the poor quality of recruits to the army during the Boer War, and along with the institution of the school medical service went a new interest in physical education, which, so far as the elementary school is concerned, really established itself at this time. In 1906 the code made allowance for organized games in school hours, and the scout and guide movements were started a few years later.

Important progress was also made in this period in a related field. A particular problem of the teacher in the board and voluntary school had been the presence in his class of children suffering from more or less severe mental or physical handicaps. Such children frequently needed an undue amount of attention, to the detriment of normal children in the class, but it was impossible to give them either the amount or quality of attention which their condition required. Quite frequently they had formed a neglected and potentially disturbing group within the class, and, since they were unable to achieve promotion, they gravitated to the lower standards where they formed a significant proportion of the children in attendance. At the same time there was an almost total absence of facilities for the teaching of children so handicapped that they could not possibly be placed in a normal school. A few enlightened school boards had provided central schools for handicapped children of various kinds. Blind and deaf children were catered for relatively early, certainly by the 1880s, and a few schools for mentally handicapped children, organized on kindergarten lines, were organized in the 1890s. But such experiments received no support from the Education Department, and it was extremely difficult to finance them since the children, obviously, earned very little in the way of grant under the Revised Code. Furthermore only the very largest boards could undertake this type of work, because smaller boards did not have enough of any particular category of child to make it economic to set up central schools. Progress only began on a national scale with the passing of the Defective and Epileptic Children Act of 1899 which empowered school boards and later local education authorities to spend public money upon special schools. Even this was only a permissive act and its requirements were only made obligatory in 1914. It was not until 1918 that its provisions were extended to physically handicapped children.

The immediate effect of the outbreak of the First World War was to delay developments in elementary education as building ceased, schools were commandeered as hospitals and barracks and teachers were called up for military service, but the long-term effect of the war is harder to analyse. There was a climate of opinion favourable to social reform, characterized by much talk of making 'a land fit for heroes to live in'.

Some important legislation resulted, the Representation of the People Act, which gave the vote to many women, the establishment of the Ministry of Health, and the Fisher Education Act of 1918. On the other hand the staggering cost of the war – about eight million pounds per day – was a major contributing factor to the recurrent economic troubles of the inter-war period, and on two occasions, in 1921 and 1931, education was to suffer severely in national economy campaigns. In spite of occasional set-backs, however, the period from 1918 to 1939 was one of rapid development for elementary schools, and it is possible to select certain aspects for particular mention here.

The first of these was the development of post-primary schooling. This is considered in greater detail in chapter 7, and here it is enough to point out that between the Wars it became general for elementary education to be reorganized so that pupils transferred from junior to senior schools at eleven years. Many local education authorities had started experiments on these lines before 1914, but reorganization was much accelerated by the Hadow Report of 1926. By 1934 half of all elementary school children over eleven years attended reorganized schools, and by 1938 two-thirds did so. The establishment of senior departments involved at least a tacit admission that the term 'elementary' school had lost much of its meaning. The distinction between the elementary and secondary systems which had been re-established by Morant after the 1902 Act was once again blurred, and there was much controversy about the relation of the two systems, a controversy which has continued in rather altered forms until the present day. The argument lay between those who thought of secondary schools as being quite distinct from the elementary schools and as essentially middle-class institutions, and those who followed R. H. Tawney in arguing that elementary and secondary education should be 'end-on' stages in the same process.

As well as losing its 'elementary' character the elementary school was ceasing to be an exclusively working-class institution. As their academic standard rose elementary schools became an attractive alternative to private schools for middle-class parents, and their attraction increased as the battle against dirt and vermin was won and as severely handicapped children were removed to special schools. During the 1920s parents who would normally be expected to send their children to private schools began to use elementary schools, not only because of their relative efficiency, but because they provided a way, through the 'scholarship' to grammar schools. Thus, in 1931, as part of a programme of national economy, 'free places' were abolished and replaced by 'special places', a sliding scale of parental contribution to fees being instituted. The new respectability of the elementary school was a quite unexpected phenomenon; it had always been taken for granted that no-one would send their children to an elementary school who could possibly afford to send them elsewhere. In the 1930s this assumption was no longer universally valid, although there was still a long way to go before it became fashionable for establishment figures to send their children to carefully chosen comprehensive schools.

The developments in teaching techniques which had begun in the Morant era accelerated after the First World War. This was partly due simply to the fact that 'payment by results' was receding into history and a new generation of teachers and administrators was rising which knew not the Revised Code. Such people were more likely than their predecessors to take the liberal views of the *Handbook of Suggestions for Teachers* at their face value. But at the same time this period was very fertile in innovations in teaching methods. Educational psychology was given a powerful impetus by Sir John Adams's popularization of Herbartian principles, and particularly by the great public interest in mental testing which arose from the development of sophisticated selection procedures during the War. Projects and variations on the Dalton plan were imported from the United States together with the teaching of John Dewey, usually as interpreted by his disciples. The child study movement, also originating in the United States reinforced the already existing tendency to take the child rather than the subject as the centre of the educational process. Acceptance of 'progressive' methods was made easier by a significant reduction in the average size of classes and an increase in the number of trained teachers. Between 1909 and 1934 the number of trained teachers rose from 97,422 to 130,654 while the school population rose by only 100,000. In 1922 there were 28,000 classes with between 50 and 60 pupils and 5,000 classes with over 60. Twelve years later these figures had been reduced to 6,138 and 56. It was no longer so absolutely necessary to use rigid methods of class control in order to obtain a measure of peace so that work could proceed.

In taking a general view of a wide historical period there is a danger of making developments appear more tidy and purposeful than they really were. When, we look, from today's standpoint, at the history of elementary education from 1800 to 1939 certain features stand out, the progressive increase in the power and influence of the government being a case in point. But it is important to realize that there are few signs of any positive government policy in educational matters before the 1902 Act, and where such a policy is discernable, as in the period when Robert Lowe was Vice-President of the Council, it was one of disengagement. Both before and after 1902 government decisions often produced quite unexpected results, while predictions of future developments, when any were made, have been inaccurate as a matter of course. Thus it appears that no contemporary realized the significance of the first Treasury grant of 1833 which was approved in an almost empty house. In 1870 it was not thought necessary to define the upper limit of elementary education, a failure of foresight which was to cause the Education Department endless trouble and eventually to lead to the 1902 Act, and the disappearance of the school boards. The failure of the Education Department to appreciate the implications of the institution of universal compulsory education is underlined by the fact that the first experiments in higher grade education were made by the Leeds School Board within two years of the passing of the 1870 Act. It was only thirty years later that the department was forced into defining the position of higher grade schools by the Cockerton Judgment. More recently the vagueness of the 1944 Act on the nature of secondary education led more or less accidentally to the adoption of what was nominally a tripartite system and to the present dispute between the supporters of selection and comprehension. Since 1944 the most careful estimates of future expansion in secondary and higher education have repeatedly been overtaken by events.

It is the untidy and unpredictable nature of the development of popular education in England which makes it unrewarding to write its history around the major reports and education acts. These were important in marking points at which changes in direction were made, but to find out why the direction was changed it is necessary to get behind the acts and reports to the aims and ambitions of pupils and teachers and to the social, political and economic pressures which bore upon them.

CHAPTER 5

CHANGES IN CURRICULA AND TEACHING
METHODS

Something has been said about the administrative changes which occurred in popular education in the period under discussion, so it is reasonable to follow with an examination of concurrent changes in curricula and teaching methods. Of course the two topics cannot be precisely distinguished. Administrative changes can have a very important influence on teaching methods; an obvious example is the introduction of the qualified assistant teacher, and the effect of 'payment by results' is notorious. For convenience of discussion, however, it is worthwhile to consider changes in curricula and teaching methods separately, with reference, where necessary, to the previous chapter.

Teachers do not approach their classes with absolutely blank minds. Even the most practical teacher, least given to theorizing about his work, plans his lessons on the basis of certain assumptions about the nature of the children in front of him, the goal of the teaching process and the best methods for attaining this goal. An examination of these assumptions helps us to understand the methods employed and to see why these methods were altered from time to time. The starting-point for this chapter, therefore, is a discussion of the assumptions upon which the monitorial system was based since the attempt to provide mass public education began with the introduction of the monitorial school. The chapter will continue by examining the factors which led to change. These factors will be considered one by one but it is important to bear in mind that changes in educational practice rarely, if ever, come about as the result of one simple cause, but are due to the pressure of several factors which become so entangled in the minds of teachers and administrators that any attempt to isolate them is bound to be somewhat artificial.

At the beginning of the nineteenth century thinking about the aims of popular education was ruled by a confused acceptance of two assumptions about child nature. Characteristically, neither of these was worked out with any rigour, which was just as well because they were really incompatible, but teachers and advocates of popular education in general succeeded in driving them in tandem.

In the first place there was a general agreement with the notion of original sin. The nature of children was thought to be essentially biased towards evil, and education was looked upon as a necessary process of redemption. If left to themselves children would, of necessity, fall into vice and crime since they lacked any inbuilt resistance to temptation, such resistance being the most important quality which education could provide.

This was an ancient and firmly established idea. John Milton wrote that 'the end of education is to repair the ruins of our first parents by virtue', while in the very year that the first monitorial school was opened Hannah More wrote that it was 'a fundamental error to consider children as innocent beings'; on the contrary, they were 'of a corrupt nature and evil dispositions'. The saying 'spare the rod and spoil the child' was taken seriously and literally. Children did not easily give up their natural tendencies, so that schooling was inevitably unpleasant and marked by frequent punishment.

Along with the notion of original sin went a belief in the omnipotence of education. This belief may be attributed to the writings of the English philospher John Locke, who flourished at the end of the seventeenth century and whose work gained enormous influence in the next hundred years. He enunciated the idea that the mind, at birth, was *tabula rasa*, a blank sheet. The child had no innate tendencies of any kind, for good or evil; his personality was the result of his experiences. The importance of this idea to educational thought is obvious. If a child's mental development is the result solely of his experience, and there are no hereditary factors, then a person who can regulate the child's environment can turn him into any kind of adult that he wishes. This gave rise to a belief in human perfectability. It was conceded that human beings were not perfect, but this was attributed to defects or deficiencies in their environment, which could, in principle at least, be remedied. Most supporters of this school believed that a child's nature was largely established in his early years, so that there were definite limits to what could be done for adults in the way of improvement. This underlined the importance of catching children while they were young and impressionable so that the next generation could be an improvement upon the present.

Clearly this was an optimistic doctrine. If heredity played a large part in people's mental make-up, then some were born bad, and that was the end of it. The teacher's task was at best a forlorn hope; he was perpetually condemned to making silk purses out of sows' ears. But if a child's nature was infinitely variable by experience the most unpromising looking material might be redeemed by skilful teaching, perhaps supported by judicious manipulation of the out-of-school environment. To a belief in this doctrine may be attributed much of the Victorian optimism about the possibility of solving the problems of poverty, vice and crime, which had been accepted as unfortunate necessities for centuries. The idea of using a prison as an institution for reforming criminals, rather than for merely keeping them out of circulation for a time was typical of this kind of thinking, as was, naturally enough, the enormous importance attached to education.

The *tabula rasa* theory had political implications which were not always clearly seen in the early nineteenth century, but which have helped to give it a new lease of life recently. It poured cold water on the idea that some men were simply born better than others – whether 'better' was construed in a moral, social or intellectual context – and averred, on the contrary, that all men were born equal in the most literal sense of the word. The thinkers of the American War of Independence and the French Revolution were, of course, influenced by this theory, and it is no coincidence that it is an article of faith in communist education.

One does not have to be a trained philosopher to see the difficulty of holding the ideas of 'original sin' and the *tabula rasa* together, since the one lays great importance on innate tendencies and the other denies their existence. Nevertheless, people are not given to working out the foundations of their thinking in great detail and the prevailing climate of opinion at the beginning of the nineteenth century favoured a moderate belief in the tendency of children to evil ways with an acceptance of the virtually unlimited power of education to form or reform character.

A second important factor in establishing the kind of schooling offered to the poor at this time was the psychological theory known as 'associationism', which held the field almost unchallenged. The essential features of associationism, for our purposes, were that it was 'atomistic' and 'mechanical'. That is to say that it pictured the mind as a kind of machine in which were associated atomic particles of meaning. Learning proceded by beginning with the simplest possible 'elements' which were stored in the mind, and it was the function of the teacher to so arrange his material that the elements were associated together in useful combinations, so that if one element were recalled, the others would be drawn from the mind after the manner of a string of sausages. In more sophisticated versions of the theory teachers were urged to look for as many different ways as possible of associating the various elements so as to facilitate meaningful recall.

It will be seen that the theory was by no means absurd, nor was it pedagogically valueless. It placed a premium on thorough preparation, and upon analysis of the material to be presented. Its weakness lay above all in its view of the pupil as a passive recipient of the material presented by the teacher. The process by which elements of knowledge became associated in the mind was thought of as entirely mechanical, engineered by the teacher's skilful organization of practice and recapitulation. No room was allowed for an active search for meaning on the part of the learner, nor for any active, if unconscious, structuring of experience on the lines suggested by Piaget. The latter omission is rather curious since the association theory achieved almost universal acceptance exactly at the time when Immanuel Kant, the German philosopher, was expounding the ideas which lie at the basis of Piaget's work. But the British were extremely slow to give any general recognition to Kant's ideas, and the belief in a mechanical, passive acceptance of impressions from the outside world dominated psychology throughout the nineteenth century.

A second important criticism of this theory as it was applied to learning was that its order of procedure was logical rather than psychological. That is to say that it assumed that the logically simplest particles of knowledge would be learned most easily, so that, to take an obvious example, one would proceed, in teaching reading, from single letters to two letter words or syllables, on to three letter words, then to four letters, then perhaps to two-syllable words, and so on. Until quite recently books for young children were often printed with the words divided into syllables – 'for read-ing by lit-tle child-ren'. The assumption was that children formed long words by building up from shorter elements. A very popular reading book at the beginning of the nineteenth century – it reached its nineteenth edition in 1816 – was written by a schoolmaster called Thomas Smith, and it exactly illustrates the effect of applying this kind of thinking. Children began by learning the alphabet, assisted by small woodcuts to illustrate each letter – A for ant, B for bell. They then graduated to learning monosyllables, reading long lists of two letter sounds, reminding one of the nonsense syllables invented by psychologists for testing memory:

Ab	eb	ib	ob	ub		
ac	ec	ic	oc	uc		
ba	be	bi	bo	bu	by	etc.

Syllables of three letters follow:

Act	asp	box	cur	dog	fin
arc	bob	cry	doe	fur	gut

At this point the pupil was introduced to simple sentences and paragraphs, and great ingenuity was shown by the author in producing entire
paragraphs of monosyllables which made sense of a kind, and which
often conveyed a moral message:

A net may rot if you let it lie in the wet, and do not set or put it by in the air to
dry. Do not cry but dry up the eye if one is nigh. Hit not the eye or toe of he who
is thy foe.

Good boys will not play with bad lads for fear they be led to be as bad as they; for
good boys may soon be made bad lads, by play-ing with such as are bad boys.

> Don't hurt a bird, or duck, or frog,
> Or lamb, or cock, or cat, or dog;
> But be you kind and show your love
> To all, and you will gain much love
> From men, and from the God a-bove.

Modern authorities on the teaching of reading are very generally
agreed that children do not, in fact, find the greatest difficulty with the
words which, to the adult mind, appear hardest to learn. The question of
interest enters the problem so that a boy may find no difficulty with a
word like 'aeroplane' or the curious word-play of the 'Cat in the Hat'
books. But interest, of course, is something of which the associationist
can take no account. His theory postulates a passive mind in which
associations are formed mechanically; active participation by the pupil in
the learning situation was at a discount.

It will be noticed that associationist psychology and belief in original
sin tended to reinforce each other, so far as teaching practice was
concerned. Co-operation between pupils and teachers was ruled out on
two counts. Children were thought of as basically inclined to evil and
therefore opposed to education, while constructive interest in learning
was ruled out by associationism. A further point is that, where a scheme
of work was based upon associationist principles, it really was very
difficult, if not impossible, for the pupil to co-operate intelligently.
Syllabuses were based upon rote learning and drill, and opportunities for
the exercise of insight or originality were minimized. Thus, as is so often
the case with theories about learning, associationism was very largely
self-confirming.

A third factor which affected the schooling offered to the poor was political. This was the chronic fear of over-educating the lower orders. Social stratification was still very rigid at the beginning of the nineteenth century, but there was sufficient movement between classes to make people very conscious of their station, and jealous of any real or imagined advantage gained by people above or, particularly, below them in the social scale. Education was offered by its advocates as a means of reconciling the lower orders to their humble role by explaining to them its political and economic necessity, but there were many who predicted, rightly as it came about, that the effect of education would not be to console them in their lot, but to inflame their feelings of injustice and suggest ways of improving it which might be very uncomfortable for their social superiors. People who argued on these lines had a powerful debating point which they frequently employed. They pointed out that many deserving members of the lower middle and working classes made substantial sacrifices in order to pay for their children's schooling. It would be unfair, so the argument continued, for other parents to have a better education provided by charity for their children. Therefore, any education which was given by charitable concerns should be of the most rudimentary kind, inferior to that obtainable in the private schools patronised by the clerks and artisans.

Fear of pauperizing the working classes reinforced this argument. There was a constant fear that the provision of free assistance to the poor, whether by private charity or from official sources, would undermine their self-respect and their willingness to provide for themselves. It was this line of thought, which is of course by no means dead at the present time, which led to the deliberate policy, especially after the new poor law of 1834, of making workhouses as unattractive as possible. Life inside them was to be only marginally better than starvation outside, so that the poor would not be tempted to a life of indolence, but would use every effort to avoid 'going on the parish'. In the same way it was believed that education should only be offered free in cases of the most extreme poverty, so as to enforce the responsibility of parents for their children. Elementary schools did, in fact, charge fees, although not on an economical scale, almost to the end of the century, a penny, twopence or threepence per week being the usual charge. When board schools ceased to levy fees it was often felt that a certain social cachet attached to attendance at Church schools where they were still paid.

For all these reasons teaching in elementary schools at the beginning of the nineteenth century was mechanical and relied to a great degree upon rote learning. Discipline was rigid and repressive and the curriculum restricted to the rudiments – reading and Bible teaching, probably but not certainly writing, and less probably some arithmetic.

The method of teaching used was the 'monitorial' system, which was absolutely universal in elementary schools from its introduction in the first years of the century until the 1840s, and very common for long afterwards, certainly until well into the school board period. Its popularity was such that it was known simply as 'the system', and was used slavishly in ludicrously unsuitable conditions.

The monitorial system was popularized at the turn of the eighteenth and nineteenth centuries by Andrew Bell and Joseph Lancaster. There was bitter controversy about who had 'invented the system, which was rather futile since there was nothing strikingly novel about the method, the chief originality lying in its universal application. The essence of the method was that the teacher did no direct teaching of the children as a whole. He selected certain of the older pupils as 'monitors' and instructed them at some convenient time, before school, at dinner time, etc. During normal school hours the monitors were each responsible for the instruction of a small group of pupils, while the teacher acted as supervisor, examiner and disciplinarian. The work was minutely sub-divided, and as soon as a group had learned one sub-division, they were tested by the teacher, before passing on to the next section. There was a complicated system of promotion and relegation both within the group and between groups, and unusual successes or lapses were rewarded by small honours or humiliations. It was the apotheosis of competition applied to the school. The organizers made some attempt to avoid the ubiquitous corporal punishment of previous schools, replacing it with the use of the dunce's cap, placards round the neck of offenders, a 'lap of honour' round the school by candidates for promotion and so on. It is a moot point whether some of the humiliations devised, particularly by Lancaster, were not more damaging in the long run than corporal punishment, but it is interesting to find a lively controversy about punishment at this early date.

The effect of the monitorial system upon the status of teachers will be considered separately, but we can examine the system here from the children's point of view. Clearly the system was devised from a point of view which equated education with the acquisition of a collection of factual knowledge. As a contemporary critic remarked, the monitors 'could instruct, they cannot educate'. At its best the system was a mechanical means of conveying elementary knowledge, but it rendered virtually impossible any direct influence of the master on the bulk of the school. Unfortunately it had a number of concealed faults which, in practice, made it even more pernicious than it, at first, appeared. One schoolmaster drew attention to the problem of procuring monitors of sufficient calibre:

From his experience does not think this system is calculated to convey efficient education: everything depends on the character of the monitors; and in populous districts, where the system, if efficient, would be best adapted to meet the demand for education, the children are withdrawn into the manufactories at such an early age that it is impossible to retain for any considerable time competent monitors. Has observed that those boys, who by their high moral character and the amount of their intellectual information, are best adapted to become monitors, have a dislike to the office on account of its retarding their own progress; while those of feebler intelligence, and with a dislike of study but also have a desire for distinction, eagerly avail themselves of the opportunity of gratifying these inclinations. The result is that the business of instruction is frequently carried on by the least qualified boys, who, although they may be more efficient than more talented individuals in maintaining discipline, are incompetent to discharge the essential duty of a teacher – that of conveying information.

Has had complaints from parents of favouritism on the part of the monitors, and is convinced that it is only through the most guarded attention on the part of the master that such a system is prevented.

The sort of mindless attention to routine which the monitorial system encouraged is demonstrated by the remarks of another teacher, less critically aware of his problems than this:

Has been master of this school for 28 years. Bell's system is adopted as nearly as possible. Has known about 20 or 30 cases in this time of monitors receiving bribes. If witness were not very vigilant thinks such cases would frequently occur. Thinks the boys make good progress with the system; and that there cannot be a better. Is not acquainted with any other system.

In the circumstances of the time it was very difficult to find a way of avoiding the monitorial system. It fitted exactly the philosophical and psychological assumptions which have already been discussed, but it also coincided with industrial considerations. It was the factory put into an educational setting. Every characteristic was there; minute division of labour; the assembly line, with children passed on from monitor to monitor until they issued complete from the top class; a complicated system of incentives to good work; an impersonal system of inspection; and finally an attention to cost-efficiency and the economic use of plant which was carried to far greater lengths than even its most modern advocates would recommend. Curiously enough the monitorial system struck upon these characteristics of modern industry long before the factory became a common feature of industrial organization, but it is not surprising that so highly organized a system should appeal to business men, and appeals by the founders of monitorial schools always emphasized their economy.

Furthermore, the economic position of the schools left the teacher very little option, as was pointed out in the last chapter. Faced by large numbers of children of every age from the nursery upwards, and with no possibility of adult assistance, the teacher was more or less compelled to group his pupils and to employ the older children to teach the younger, and the monitorial system was simply a regularization of this position. There was also a contributory factor which is not commonly appreciated. Schools, prior to the introduction of the monitorial system, were rarely very large; twenty to forty pupils was a fair average. These schools were organized on a method of individual teaching, each child having separate work to do, the teacher sitting at his desk and correcting their work as they completed it; any illustration of a seventeenth- or eighteenth-century school will show this system at work.

In a small school this was a perfectly rational method of procedure, but elementary schools in the nineteenth century became very large, 250 pupils to one master was nothing out of the ordinary, and schools of 500 or more pupils were known. With such numbers individual teaching was out of the question and the school needed to be closely organized if any work were to be done; the alternative was chaos, and the evidence suggests that this was the condition of many schools. One investigator remarked in 1842: 'Several of the schools which I have visited were in a state approaching the riotous, and so little control had the masters, that it was only amidst incessant interruptions and confusion that the information sought could be obtained.' Only with the introduction of David Stow's 'simultaneous system' of teaching was a viable alternative to monitorial organisation found. This approximated to the modern idea of class teaching, with the teacher instructing the whole class at once – hence the 'simultaneous' system, but it required the division of the school into classes, and the provision of adequate assistant teachers before it could be generally adopted, and this, as was observed in the previous chapter, was not practical politics until the school board period.

For three-quarters of the nineteenth century teaching methods in elementary schools did not change very much. The introduction of the pupil-teacher[1] in 1846 did much to raise the quality of the teaching which became rather less mechanical and allowed for more direct contact

---

[1] See below, chapter 6.

between teacher and pupil. But these were changes of detail; the same assumptions were made, but the application was rather more enlightened.

To a degree this was due to very practical considerations. Improvements in teacher training were largely cancelled out by greatly increased classes – a familiar educational phenomenon – while 'payment by results' put an abrupt stop to attempts to liberalize the teaching. The Revised Code of 1862, however, demonstrates the major reason for the slow rate of change; there was no real change, except in a few unusually enlightened people, in the assumptions which guided educational practice. Teaching was still looked upon as the mechanical passing on of inert facts to passive recipients, while Robert Lowe, the author of the code, gave the classic enunciation of the argument[1] that the poor should receive a limited education, quite different from that of the rich, and fitting them for their humble station in life. Until these assumptions were questioned no radical changes in teaching methods or curricula were to be expected, and it is the function of the rest of this chapter to examine the factors which led to the questioning, and to the abandoning, in part at least, of these assumptions. These factors rarely worked in isolation; they inter-acted vigorously, and in this analysis they are only treated separately for convenience of discussion.

The first factor to consider was a change of the views relating to child nature. This change is generally referred to the writing of Jean-Jacques Rousseau, as interpreted by such practical educators as Pestalozzi and Froebel, but in fact it is to be seen in the work and writings of a very large number of educators from at least the beginning of the eighteenth century onwards, and as often as not it appears to spring from a teacher's experience of a discrepancy between the accepted theory and the observed behaviour of children. In particular teachers discovered that, given the opportunity, children could show an interest in their work, and a degree of responsibility which could not be equated with a belief in their innate tendency towards evil.

If the new 'child-centred' approach were adopted, children were seen as basically good and only corrupted by society – a direct contradiction of the older belief. Several important implications for practice were to be found in this doctrine. It became relevant to work from the children's interests, and the interest of the class became a criterion of good teaching, whereas before it had been quite irrelevant. The co-operation of the class could be looked for, and, in fact, the emphasis was on

[1] See above, p. 25.

self-development, the teacher acting in a far less dominating manner, assisting the learner to find his way, rather than pressing him forward along a previously determined route. Childhood became of importance in itself, and was not merely a stage in the development towards the desirable state of adulthood. Far less emphasis, therefore, could be placed upon preparation as a motive for education and more upon personal education than upon the requirements of society.

The 'child-centred' approach took a long time to penetrate to the elementary school. Several private schools, however, were experimenting with co-operation with their pupils and in allowing them a measure of responsibility before the end of the eighteenth century, and there were many cases, a little later, of schools where the pupils ran their own social and athletic clubs and even had some responsibility for discipline. It was possible for head-teachers to go a long way in this direction without being fully committed to the child-centred philosophy. In fact it is likely that most English experimenters in this field arrived at their ideas from an analysis of their own experience, and without much thought for their theoretical foundations. Where this was the case they might well accept certain 'child-centred' notions while totally rejecting, or being ignorant of, others. Thus Thomas Arnold, a strong believer in education as preparation, took an important part in breaking down the idea of a 'natural' hostility between teacher and taught.

The result of adopting this approach was a change in attitude rather than in subjects. A man like Arnold could be an ardent classicist while pioneering the giving of responsibility to his senior pupils. The main influence of the 'child-centred' school on curricula lay in its idea of teaching 'children rather than subjects', in emphasizing, that is to say, the non-academic side of education. Under the existing system education was almost entirely intellectual; no attention was paid to aesthetic or physical aspects, and until well into the nineteenth century surprisingly little was done in the direction of moral education beyond catechism and undirected biblical instruction. HMIs and other observers repeatedly remarked on the total ineffectiveness of such teaching in spite of the length of time spent upon it. The work of 'child-centred' writers and teachers did something to prepare the ground for the great expansion of the curriculum which occurred in the second half of the nineteenth century by urging the claims to consideration of physical, emotional and cultural factors.

The demand for the introduction of new subjects appeared first in the secondary field, and only became relevant when elementary schools began to attempt work of a secondary nature in the 1880s. Until this time elementary schools were fully occupied in teaching the rudiments, and a negligible amount of more advanced work was attempted. It is doubtful whether the standard of work done in elementary schools increased very much before the school board period; in fact those in a position to know were of the opinion that the standard might be actually falling, because of the large numbers of totally ignorant children who were being brought into the schools by successive crusades for attendance. After a century and a half in which standards of work have invariably been seen to be falling we may have reason to be sceptical of the more pessimistic assessments of the work in elementary schools at this period, but it is quite certain that the curriculum of elementary schools in 1870 was virtually identical with that of thirty or forty years earlier. What little progress was made in the years following the introduction of pupil-teachers, in 1846, was cut off short by the Revised Code of 1862.

From at least as early as the middle of the eighteenth century, secondary-school teachers had been concerned to devise what even in those days was called a 'liberal education'. There was not yet any very general call for technical training at a secondary level; this was still provided by apprenticeship, which survived in the professions and what would later be called 'white collar' jobs, long after it was virtually defunct among craftsmen. The particular problem was to find a course of study suitable for a boy – and occasionally a girl – who would leave school at fourteen or sixteen and go into a bank, office or warehouse. Private school proprietors, who were particularly exercised by this question, saw clearly enough that the Classics would not answer. Whatever their merits, they were dead languages, and the pupils at their schools very rarely remained long enough to get beyond grammar to a study of classical literature. In addition parents were sufficiently influenced by the 'utilitarian' philosophers to demand a 'useful' education for their sons, and private schools were, by their nature, extremely susceptible to consumer demand.

The result of the experiments of many teachers was the appearance in the curriculum of the 'modern subjects', English, modern languages, history, geography, the sciences, mathematics and the numerous vocational subjects, shorthand, commercial writing, surveying, navigation, etc. English was taught through grammar as a dead language, which was curious since foreign languages were almost always taught colloquially by the direct method. Every private school of any pretensions, for example, engaged peripatetic foreigners to teach their native language. Frequent revolutions on the Continent provided a ready supply of educated foreigners willing to make a living in this way. Teachers often introduced practical work into mathematics at first, but the subject was treated with less flexibility and imagination as it became more usual, and the same occurred with other new subjects. Very probably the early teachers of these subjects were enthusiasts with a certain missionary zeal which was missing in their followers who merely followed an established syllabus.

These subjects began to filter into elementary schools in the 1830s and 1840s but were only taken by a very few of those children who stayed at school longest. Their educational value was very slight, partly because of the low standard of the teaching and partly because the children were unready for work in subjects which had never been properly analysed as teaching instruments. Far the most popular of the 'modern' subjects in elementary schools were English grammar, which was taught in a soul-destroying imitation of the worst kind of Latin gerund-grinding, history and geography. The weakness of geography, then and for long afterwards, was its total lack of relation to the experience of the child.

When a country is pointed out by name to him upon the map, and he has learned to tell how in respect to the four cardinal points it is bounded by other countries, and what are the names of its rivers and mountains, and chief towns, his memory may have been largely taxed, and yet his principal idea of the country may, nevertheless, remain in a great degree, identified with an irregular figure upon a piece of paper. A vast chasm is interposed in the child's mind between the objects with which he is himself familiar and those which, in such instruction, he is required to conceive the existence; a chasm which his imagination is not strong enough to bear him over.

About history one of the first HMIs remarked:

There is this remarkable characteristic in the knowledge of English history among National school children that rarely does it extend down to the present time. It is frequently limited to those apocryphal periods which precede the Conquest, and seldom extends beyond the reign of Henry VIII or Elizabeth. It is begun at the beginning, but never finished.

In fact, it was not until the 1880s that the elementary school curriculum really began to widen and deepen. Then, rather rapidly, new subjects were introduced and the standard of work rose sharply. Some facts and figures will illustrate the suddenness of this development. In 1873 the average attendance at recognized elementary schools in Nottingham was rather more than 7,000, and in that year only 610 children were presented for examination in work beyond the three 'Rs'. This may be an exaggeration since there is no way of knowing whether or not some children were presented in more than one subject, only the number of passes being recorded. In the next few years the Code allowed for an extension of the curriculum by paying a special grant to schools where 'class subjects' were taught in addition to the three 'Rs'. In 1880 3,570 Nottingham children qualified for this payment, which was only available for senior pupils in Standard IV and above, while 708 passes were obtained in 'specific subjects', another addition authorized under the Code and 802 passes in the drawing examinations of the Science and Art Department. By 1895 the position was totally different: 11,306 pupils passed the drawing examinations, and 7,821 took 'specific subjects'. Substantial grants were earned by numerous schools in science subjects examined by the Science and Art Department. But the greatest innovation was the introduction of classes in wood and metalwork – known as manual work – and in practical cookery, and of demonstrations of scientific experiments. The manual work and cookery had to be pressed forward in the face of determined opposition by the Education Department and often by local ratepayers, and it was never possible to offer more than an hour or so every other week to senior pupils. Likewise the science consisted of a lecture and demonstration once a fortnight given by peripatetic demonstrators who pushed their apparatus from school to school on handcarts.

Experiments like these were clearly only a tentative beginning. The emphasis remained very much on the three 'Rs', and science, manual work, cookery and drawing were 'extras' very liable to be cut in time of economy. It was only in schools run by the largest school boards that such experiments were conducted; smaller boards could not afford the expense nor find the specialist teachers to do much more than teach the rudiments. Nevertheless, even in the small rural schools there was a rise in standards and some widening of the curriculum for senior pupils.

It was during the school board period that one of the most important factors leading to extension of the curriculum made its appearance. This was the demand of pupils who had completed the standard course of the elementary school for more advanced work.[1] Originally the government code allowed for six standards, raised in 1880 to seven, but from the late 1870s children began to remain at school in large numbers after they had passed through all the standards. It was this development which produced the higher grade schools, where senior pupils from several elementary schools were gathered together at one centre for advanced work. In the higher grade schools there were interesting experiments with curricula of a vocational and semi-vocational type. Unfortunately

[1] See also above, chapter 2, pp. 36–7.

these experiments were cut short by the machinations of Sir Robert Morant, who, as effective head of the Board of Education brought out regulations for secondary education which had a strongly literary bias.

Higher grade schools are best considered under the heading of secondary education, but the same influences which led to their establishment were operating within the ordinary elementary school. With the introduction, and enforcement, of compulsory schooling, attendance became regular and children remained at school for longer. In the 1840s a school could expect to have an average attendance of 60 per cent of the children on the register, and the average school life was a fraction under two years. By the 1890s children were staying at school for a minimum of six years and attendance had risen to over 90 per cent. It was only to be expected that standards should rise and the curriculum be widened.

During the school board period there was a rapid rise in interest in education as a national investment, due partly to fear of foreign industrial competition and partly to concern about Britain's political situation.[1] The direct effect on the work of elementary schools was not very great, but the high level of interest in education made public opinion inclined to accept a relatively large expenditure on schools, which allowed school boards to make great improvements in staffing and equipment. There was also a surge of interest in technical training, and the large school boards, with London usually in the van, produced extensive schemes for evening classes in technical and commercial subjects. These were often arranged in conjunction with the new municipal universities – Leeds, Birmingham, Nottingham, Sheffield, etc. – which were more like technical colleges in their early days than the present-day idea of a university. This interest in technical education has, of course, been a more or less constant factor ever since, and, by and large, the British response has always been to keep technical training out of the secondary school, and to delay it until the tertiary stage.

An influence on the curriculum very much related to the requirements of industry and business was the rise of the competitive examination. Until the nineteenth century entry into business and government posts, and promotion once inside, depended upon what the sociologists call 'sponsored mobility', which may be translated as 'the old school tie'. Under the circumstances this was not an absurd method. Whether locally or nationally, the number of applicants for any post was limited, and the man making the appointment either knew the candidates personally, or was acquainted with someone who did. There was, of course, a great deal

[1] See above, chapter 2, pp. 32–3.

of favouritism and downright nepotism, but where the field was limited and known to the appointing panel there was no particular objection to the system as such. At the time there was certainly no objection on the grounds of favouritism or patronage since it was regarded as a virtue on the part of an important personage that he looked after his dependents in the distribution of offices.

In the early nineteenth century three objections were raised to sponsored mobility. First, the ethics of patronage were questioned, and a search was begun for a method of selection which avoided the personal factor. Second, with the increasing population and a relaxing of class boundaries, the pool of possible candidates for office was much enlarged, and it became increasingly difficult to discover reliable information about many of them. This difficulty was enhanced by a great increase in geographical mobility, especially with the coming of the railway, which meant that there might be a national response to advertisement for quite minor posts. Third, as legislators and business men became increasingly concerned about foreign competition, they wished to widen the field of selection still further so as to be sure that men of talent were not passed over because of their lack of connections. The careers of men like Arkwright, Telford, the Stephensons, Brunel, drove home the message that many such men existed if an instrument could be found to identify them.

The instrument which was produced was the competitive examination, which, as W. S. Gilbert pointed out in *Iolanthe* became something of a later Victorian fetish, like the 'objective test' of more recent years – and for very similar reasons. The Indian and home civil services pioneered the idea, but were soon followed by the armed forces and numerous official or unofficial bodies. Along with independent entrance examinations appeared public examinations which could be used for qualifying purposes. A pass in such an examination gave a candidate publicly verifiable credentials which had currency all over the country, and parents and teachers were quick to realize the advantages of directing their pupils towards them. By the end of the century private, higher grade and the newly revived grammar schools were working for such examinations as the College of Preceptors Leaving Certificate, the Oxford and Cambridge Local Examinations, the London University Matriculation – very popular with teachers – and various qualifications offered by the Royal Society of Arts. The main effect of this on the schools was to standardize the curriculum. Whether they wished to do so or not the examiners found themselves laying down the syllabuses of work, and there can be little doubt that the effect of gearing syllabuses to the requirements of an examination frequently meant that the work done possessed very little intrinsic value.

The examination problem struck elementary schools rather later than secondary schools. Some school boards already had examinations for selecting pupils for higher grade schools in the 1880s, but the 'scholarship' really became significant after 1907 when the 'free place' system was introduced. Especially after the First World War the competition for places was very intense, and coaching for the 'scholarship' was done on a large scale. Once again the requirements of examination tended to dictate the syllabus.

From early in the twentieth century curricula and methods were much influenced by the ideas of the American philosophers of the 'pragmatic' school, and particularly by the teaching of John Dewey. The pragmatists looked for a justification for teaching a subject in its usefulness, and they rejected the notion of a hierarchy of subjects. The classics had come to be defended on the grounds that they provided a valuable 'mental training'. As physical exercise trained the body, so Latin trained the mind, and once trained it could be turned equally well to a variety of uses. If this were true it would obviously be economical to concentrate upon the Classics, since the trained mind of a classicist could easily be provided with the technical knowledge upon which its powerful intelligence could operate. The result of this line of thinking was that the Classics were firmly established at the top of the hierarchy of subjects because of their general application while other, technical, subjects occupied a subordinate position. This was still very much the accepted doctrine when Morant drew up the regulations for secondary schools in 1904, which were the death blow to the vocationally biased higher grade schools. Such schools were admitted to be useful for artisans, but a real secondary education could only be gained through the mental training of the Classics.

The American thinkers rejected the whole idea of mental training and carried out experiments to prove their point. These experiments were of very dubious validity, but the mental training theory, as developed at the beginning of the twentieth century, rested on no scientific foundations whatsoever, and psychologists like William James were easily able to expose this fact. The pragmatists argued that every subject must stand on its own merits, and, since virtually any subject can be shown to be useful, this gave a respectable philosophical justification for a vast expansion of the curriculum. This was never carried very far in Britain, where mental training, usually in its less extreme and more defensible forms, has retained a strong hold. In the USA, however, the curriculum became seriously fragmented, and since the Second World War there has been an important reaction in the direction of a 'core curriculum' comprising certain subjects thought to be of basic importance. In very recent years the doctrine of 'mental training' has enjoyed a strong revival, although in a much more sophisticated form, and it is interesting to find American psychologists among its strongest exponents.

Pragmatism was also important in its effect on the relations between teacher and pupil. Dewey and his followers were strongly democratic in their sympathies and believed that if the school was to prepare children for democratic society it must be a democratic society itself. This was by no means a novel idea; experiments in democratic organization, especially in private schools were fairly common in the nineteenth century and known in the eighteenth. After the First World War, however, it became common form to condemn 'authoritarianism' in teachers and to recommend co-operation and consultation with the pupils. The effect of this was to reinforce the importance attached by the 'child centred' school to the interest of the learner. Apart from leading to a less formal teacher-pupil relationship, this encouraged experiments in such methods as projects and the Dalton plan, which depended upon the initiative of the learner. On the other hand there was much criticism of more traditional methods by which information was dispensed by the teacher to a passive class.

These changes were hastened by developments in psychological theories. The associationist doctrine, which held the field in English educational thinking throughout the nineteenth century, was challenged by various theories which allowed a more positive role to the learner. Instead of being regarded as the passive recorder of information, the pupil was looked upon as actively organizing and selecting the material with which he was supplied. Attention was transferred from the teacher to the learner, and teaching considered as a process of so shaping the child's environment that the optimum conditions obtained for learning. So far as possible the child was to be put into the position of a discoverer rather than a receiver of knowledge. An important by-product of this way of thinking was that the emphasis shifted from knowledge of facts to knowledge of techniques of enquiry. It was not regarded as so important to be knowledgeable as to know where the knowledge was to be found. All these ideas, of course, fitted in very well with the pragmatic philosophy, which placed a high value on activity compared with knowledge. Mere knowledge, as such, was valueless; it acquired value in its application.

At the beginning of the chapter it was pointed out that curricula and teaching methods reflect assumptions which are held by teachers about child nature, the aims of education, and so on. In the course of a century and a half these assumptions have changed and concurrent changes have occurred in methods and schemes of work. So far as the average teacher is concerned, these assumptions are largely unconscious; few people other than philosophers, have the time or inclination to analyse the foundations of their thinking. From our point of view it is possible to exaggerate the importance of individual innovators. More significant is the half-conscious acceptance by ordinary teachers of eclectic versions of new educational ideas. The influence of 'child centred' notions was far wider than the group of teachers who were formal advocates of that school of thought. It lay in the slow, but eventually almost universal, acceptance of childhood as a stage of life with values of its own, and of the interests of children as being a relevant criterion of good teaching. In the same way activity methods and democratic classroom organization are applied by numerous teachers who have scarcely heard of, still less read, Dewey and Kilpatrick.

CHAPTER 6

THE ROLE AND STATUS OF THE TEACHER

Before discussing developments in the teacher's role and status in detail, it is necessary to specify the class of people under consideration. Discussions on this topic are frequently vitiated by confusion between the 'schoolmaster' and the 'teacher', and it is as well to clarify this point in advance. In this context a 'schoolmaster' is taken to be a man teaching in a public, independent or grammar school, or in one of the fashionable private academies. He was certainly a graduate, teaching academic subjects, and in the nineteenth century probably a clergyman. In the kind of school in which the 'schoolmaster' taught a distinction was usually made until very recently between the graduate academic staff and the 'instructors' in practical subjects or physical education, who occupied a lower position in the hierarchy. The status of 'schoolmasters' was closely geared to that of the clergy – in so far as the two groups are distinguishable. That is to say that their status rose rapidly from the early eighteenth century until the end of the nineteenth. This process can be seen by comparing the attitude towards the clergyman expressed in the novels of, for example, Fielding, Austen and Dickens. In the present century the financial and social position of the 'schoolmaster' has declined sharply, so that the distinction between the 'schoolmaster' and the 'teacher' has become blurred.

The 'teacher', in this chapter, is a man or woman teaching in elementary schools or the schools which have descended from the elementary school. In the early nineteenth century it was impossible to draw a clear line between private teachers in cheap day schools and teachers in 'public' schools, in the American sense, and both groups will be discussed here, where relevant.

The treatment will in general be chronological, but it is necessary to extract one theme for separate mention. Throughout the period there has been a dispute about whether to regard teaching as a vocation or as a profession, and this has affected the status of the teacher – and of the schoolmaster – and has had a particular bearing on the questions of training and salaries. There has always been a feeling that teachers are born, not made, and that a 'real' teacher feels a strong sense of vocation. This leads, naturally enough, to placing a low value upon training, and to a feeling that the question of income is rather irrelevant. In the case of the schoolmaster this feeling was reinforced by the curious English admiration for the cultured amateur, and independent schools have never come round to a belief in the usefulness of training for teaching.

The attitude towards the teacher was different. There was no question of the cultured amateur in this case. But Kay-Shuttleworth, who had more to do than anyone else with establishing elementary school teaching as a recognized occupation, was a keen student of Continental innovators who drew their inspiration from Pestalozzi. From them he accepted two notions. First, he thought of the elementary school teacher as a missionary serving among the poor, and therefore he looked for a sense of religious vocation. At the same time he was afraid that the teacher might be divorced from the social class he was engaged in teaching, and was much concerned to inculcate a feeling of humility among student teachers. This second motive fitted in well with the chronic fear, which has been observed before, of over-educating the working classes. For both reasons Kay-Shuttleworth and his followers were only interested in providing a scale of pay equivalent to that of an artisan, and were inclined to think of training for teaching in terms of a craft apprenticeship rather than as preparation for a profession. It is only in very recent times that this view of the teacher's role has been seriously challenged, and it still enjoys considerable support – not least among teachers themselves.

It is difficult to characterize briefly the status of teachers at the beginning of the nineteenth century, since the term covered such a variety of people. Before the appearance of the monitorial schools of the National and British Societies public provision of schools for the mass of the working class was virtually non-existent. Schooling was provided by private enterprise, and this naturally meant that the poor tended to get the worst schools. Private school proprietors who made a success of their trade generally raised their fees and aimed at a higher class of client, whose trade was more profitable. There was a process of natural selection at work and many of the proprietors of respectable writing schools or academies started their career with little day schools for the children of artisans.

There is evidence that some at least of the proprietors of private schools for the poor were regarded as respectable men and women with a skill to sell. When Sunday schools were first established, in the 1780s and 1790s, the founders frequently contracted with such people to run the schools at so much per child. The men who founded the Sunday schools were of a distinctly puritan frame of mind and would have been very disinclined to have made such agreements with men of dubious character.

On the other hand it was far too easy to set oneself up as a teacher. All that one needed was a room. Even quite flourishing schools were one room affairs with perhaps twenty or thirty pupils, and few had any equipment worth talking about. Many teachers ran little schools as a part-time supplement to some other occupation; bakers, cobblers, stonemasons, weavers, shop-keepers, all followed this practice. Numerous women ran schools for pin-money, and these in particular were often no more than baby-minding institutions. It was a common practice for men and women to decline into teaching after failing in other professions, and there is no reason to suppose that they were better at teaching than at anything else. A case occurs in the diary of the Rev. James Woodforde, for 1762, which illustrates this process of decline and also the current assessment of the trade of teacher:

Papa had a letter from cousin James Lewis at Nottingham wherein he informs us that he kept a little school at Nottingham, and likewise is in great need of money. He was a private soldier in the army, and being wounded in the leg rendered him unserviceable, and therefore he had a pension of £5 per annum from the government; he has been rather wild in his time, which has brought him to this.

The introduction of the monitorial system tended, if anything, to depress the teacher's status still further. The standard of work remained abysmally low and was rendered even more monotonous and mechanical, and the fact that the actual teaching was done by child monitors raised questions about the amount of skill involved in the activity. If it could be successfully performed by children, why go to the expense of paying a qualified adult? The training given to a teacher, where any training occurred at all, emphasized the unskilled nature of his trade. He usually spent a short period – a week or two was considered adequate – attached to the school of an experienced teacher. This time was occupied by the student in spending a day with each group of children, following an accelerated course through the school. Alternatively an 'organizing master' was sent to a new school to initiate the intending teacher into 'the system'. As soon as 'the system' had been acquired the organizing master went on his way to the next school.

The emphasis on 'the system' – which meant the monitorial system – was one of the two factors which did most to keep the status of the teacher low in this period. The system was accepted with a quite uncritical enthusiasm and the measure of a teacher was the accuracy with which he applied it; any deviation was looked upon as heresy. A result of this attitude of mind was that the teacher was regarded as merely the rather unimportant agent of an infallible organization, and his individual skill was reckoned a negligible factor in the school's success. The whole aim of the monitorial school was to reduce the need for adult teachers, and the logical conclusion was to manage without an adult teacher at all. Certainly the test of a good monitorial school was that it ran in the most mechanical manner possible and with the minimum of intervention by the teacher.

The eternal problem of elementary schools in this period was poverty. Their budgets were astonishingly small. In one large new British school the total income for its first year, when subscribers were still being energetically canvassed, was £131 12s. 11d., from which two teachers had to be paid. Another British school in the same town raised £62 14s. 3d., while the national school had an income of £111 12s. 6d. These were relatively flourishing institutions in a populous area; most schools had to manage on even more limited resources than these. The result of this poverty was that the income – in the words of a contemporary Parliamentary commission – was too low

to secure the zealous services of properly trained and qualified teachers . . . While such pittance, in many cases less than the wages of an intelligent workman, continues to be paid, it will be in vain to expect efficient teachers. With no encouragement for exertion – no promotion for good conduct, it is not surprising that masters so situated should be looking for other, and more profitable, employment. The consequence is that educated persons will not undertake the office, which but too generally is filled by men who have failed in other occupations.

The average pay of teachers in National and British schools in the Midland area at this time was as follows:

Masters	£51 15s. 3d.	About half the
Mistresses	£28 19s. 0d.	teachers were
Infant mistresses	£18 6s. 1d.	provided with a house.

These averages are probably quite useful guides. One master in the Midland area is recorded as having an income of £105, but he was an exception; £80–£90 was a good salary for the master of a big town school, £45–£60 was considered about right for a suburban or rural school, which would usually be much smaller. The pay of mistresses was far lower, but it is known that many of the lowest salaries were, in practice, supplemented by a share of the fees. A case is recorded of a mistress whose salary, returned as £25, was raised to £60 by her share of the school pence. This made her almost the highest paid mistress in the area.

The teachers' poverty was aggravated by their lack of prospects. There was virtually no chance of a rise in salary, however efficient the teacher was. In fact the reverse was the case, since schools frequently found their incomes declining as they lost their novelty and had to economize. Since the teacher's salary represented at least three-quarters of the total outlay of the school, he was obliged to either accept a cut in pay or try for another school elsewhere, and as he became older, so this became more difficult. It was by no means exceptional for this to occur; the evidence suggests that most schools had to economise in this way at some time, while some were in chronic financial straits throughout their career. There was, of course, no pension scheme; a teacher had to continue in his post until he was quite unable to do so – often long after he had ceased to be efficient, and it was quite impossible for him to make any significant savings out of his miserable income.

In 1846, chiefly due to the efforts of Sir James Kay-Shuttleworth, the pupil-teacher system was introduced. To all intents and purposes the profession of elementary school teacher dates from this event, since it provided for a supervized training leading to a recognized qualification, which carried with it a salary partly guaranteed by the government. There was even a pension scheme, although this was later revoked. Under the pupil-teacher system a boy or girl was apprenticed to a teacher, usually at the age of thirteen, and he served for five years, taking an examination, set by the visiting HMI, every year. Upon passing each year's examination the pupil-teacher received a small stipend, his teacher receiving a supplement to his salary from the government. When he completed his articles the pupil teacher sat for the Queen's Scholarship, and those who finished high on the list were eligible for a scholarship tenable at one of the training colleges. Whether or not a pupil-teacher proceded to college, he became a qualified teacher with a government certificate – known as his 'parchment'. The certificates were issued in different classes, and it was possible for the class to be raised at intervals upon a series of favourable reports by HMI at the annual inspection.

There were regulations governing the number of apprentices that any teacher might take, and the hours of instruction which had to be given. This instruction, which followed a rigidly structured syllabus, was given out of normal school hours, and it covered both academic work and what would now be called 'education'. When the apprentices were not being instructed they helped in the school. Naturally the work they were expected to do depended upon the stage they had reached, but older

103

pupil-teachers spent most of their time teaching, generally with groups of pupils in the 'classrooms'. It was assumed that pupil-teachers would be a liability to the teacher in their early days, but would repay him as they became more experienced.

The strain, both on teacher and upon apprentice, of this half-time system was very great, and various attempts were made in the late nineteenth century, by the larger school boards, to find a way of easing it. These invariably involved reducing the time a pupil-teacher spent teaching and approximating his training to a secondary school education. Pupil-teacher centres were established, which were secondary schools in all but name, and these dominated the Queen's Scholarship, because of the facilities they offered to their students to reach a high academic level. The advantages of separating the intending teacher's secondary education from his technical training were so obvious that, in 1909, the government introduced an alternative scheme, whereby candidates were allotted a bursary tenable at a secondary school, followed by a grant to attend a training college. From this date the pupil-teacher system rapidly lost ground, but it survived in authorities which were not prepared to provide the necessary secondary school places until after the Second World War.

The pupil-teacher system provided a solution to both the great problems which blocked the way to the establishment of a teaching profession. It gave to the successful apprentice a recognized certificate of technical competence, and it made it possible for the intending teacher to raise his own educational standard – and the ignorance of elementary school teachers had long been a scandal. The system was greeted with warm approval by the people who were best placed to assess its results. One HMI remarked:

If there is one part of the present measures in operation for the improvement of the labouring classes more satisfactory and full of hope than another, it is the system of apprenticeship by which a large body of teachers are now being trained . . . I think it would be difficult to find a number of young men and women who have given greater satisfaction or whose conduct has been more exemplary.

The aim of the pupil-teacher system to raise the academic standard of elementary school teachers was not unchallenged. There were those who argued, first, that the level of work done in such schools was so low that high academic achievements would be wasted, and second, that the pupil-teachers would be given ideas above their station. This was one manifestation of the recurrent fear of the effects of education upon the 'lower orders', and it was crushingly answered by Matthew Arnold, then an HMI:

It is sufficient to say that the plan which these objectors recommend, the plan of employing teachers whose attainments do not rise far above the level of the attainments of their scholars, has already been tried. It has tried and it has failed. Its fruits were to be seen in the condition of elementary education throughout England until a very recent period. It is now sufficiently clear that the teacher to whom you give only a drudge's training, will do only a drudge's work, and will do it in a drudge's spirit.

As the pupil-teacher system spread, elementary school teaching became a certificated profession. In 1852 there were 52 certificated teachers and 185 pupil-teachers in the Midland area in national schools; by 1861 the numbers were 416 and 671 respectively. Since the qualified assistant teacher was still virtually unknown – there were only three adult assistants in the area in 1855 – this meant that some 400 schools had a qualified teacher in charge.

These teachers soon began to show signs of professional consciousness. By the middle of the 1850s local associations of teachers were quite common; they were partly social in nature, but also held meetings to hear lectures and discuss educational topics. One such association produced its own manuscript magazine. Some at least of these local associations enjoyed a measure of recognition as negotiating bodies. In 1869 the Nottingham and Nottinghamshire Church Schoolmaster's Association was able to persuade the Archdeacon and the local HMI to stop the custom of publishing a list of each school's percentage of passes in the annual examination, and it is interesting to see that both sides in the negotiation accepted the association as enjoying a representative status.

As teaching became a recognizable profession the pay of teachers improved significantly. By 1855 the average salary of a certificated master in the Midland area was £87 per year; certificated mistresses received about £57. In other words there was an improvement of at least 60 per cent and there was also a marked increase in the number of teachers who were provided with a house. The standard school design recommended by the Education Department always included a teacher's house, but since most schools had two departments – boys and girls – and many had an infants' department in addition, there were never enough houses to go round. In 1855 about half of all certificated teachers had a school-house, which represented a substantial addition to their income, and this figure was never improved upon, because from this time qualified assistants began to appear and these were never given a house.

By this time the certificated elementary school teacher had established himself among that aristocracy of the working class who are recorded by E. J. Hobsbawm as earning wages in the region of 28s. to £2 per week. They therefore joined the proprietors of the middle range of private schools, who had always been among the more articulate and politically conscious members of the working class, and it is interesting to notice that the Labour party, and the various organizations of working men which preceeded it recruited many energetic workers from the ranks of elementary school teachers. Teachers, of course, had certain advantages over members of trades which enjoyed similar status. The possibility of receiving a school-house was one, but there was also the stability of a teacher's job, which was not subject to fluctuations in the state of trade in the way that a skilled craftsman's job might be. A fact which became increasingly important towards the end of the century, however, was that the kind of education a teacher received fitted him for posts outside the teaching profession which commanded more attractive salaries, and the drain of men from teaching became a serious problem.

With the appearance of the Revised Code in 1862 a new feature appeared which altered the teachers' pay scale. It now became usual to pay the teacher on a commission basis, with a basic salary and a fraction of the government grant earned by the scholars. The intention, obviously, was to provide an incentive to teachers to produce good results at the annual examination and thereby increase the grant. The payment of teachers on this basis was virtually universal for about thirty years, and was given up in the 1890s, the larger school boards leading the way, under pressure from the teachers' organizations. But although the system was used everywhere it was applied in very varying ways, and it tended to widen the gap, which already existed, between the relative affluence of urban teachers and the poverty of rural teachers. Thus, in 1875, when the Nottingham School Board drew up its first pay scale it stipulated that head-teachers should receive (for men) £110–£130 plus one third of the grant, and for women, £70–£80 plus one-quarter of the grant. In a large village just across the river from Nottingham the mistress was paid £70 plus one-twentieth of the grant, a far less generous arrangement, but typical of the scale of pay for rural head-teachers. Since the grant for quite a moderately sized urban school in the 1870s, would amount to at least £150, it will be seen that one-third of the grant represented a very attractive bonus.

The establishment of a qualified profession undoubtedly meant a distinct levelling up in standards. The appointment of a qualified teacher was a guarantee that a certain minimum standard would be reached, and no more is heard of teachers who were disreputable and scandalously incompetent. But the system had its limitations. It tended to produce teachers who were competent, but uninspired and undisposed towards originality and experiment. This characteristic was noted at the time.

'Ranging the schools I have inspected under the headings of "good", "fair", and "indifferent", I find this year, as in former years, the second of these classes far the most numerous. Much of the instruction they exhibit is satisfactory; but it is marked by a constant tendency to fall into a groove.' It was inevitable that the pupil-teacher system should produce this result since it allowed virtually no opportunity for the apprentice to study methods beyond the confines of his own school, and he could hardly be expected to examine education in its wider context. The pupil-teacher's experience was entirely confined to elementary schools, and even if he went to college he mixed entirely with students whose experience was similarly limited. Perhaps the greatest weakness of the system was this self-perpetuating character, but in the mid-nineteenth century there was no way in which working-class children could have their education at secondary schools subsidized, so that there was really no alternative to pupil-teaching.

The tendency of teachers to favour rule-of-thumb, unadventurous methods was confirmed by the Revised Code, with its emphasis on the achievement of measurable results in a limited field. So far as teachers were concerned the results of the Revised Code were entirely unfortunate. There was a return to the drill and minute sub-division of material which had marked the monitorial system; experiments in widening the curriculum were cut off short. Relations between teachers and inspectors received a set-back from which they have never fully recovered, and teachers were put in the position of being forced to attempt to deceive the inspectors in order to earn their living. But perhaps the longest lived legacy of 'payment by results' was the importance given to petty administration, which has plagued teachers – particularly head teachers – ever since. This cannot be blamed entirely upon the Revised Code; school boards and local education authorities soon developed an insatiable appetite for forms and returns. But the pattern was set by the requirements of the education department, which included, for example, the instruction that the teacher's first duty in case of fire was to rescue the register. This regulation, surely the apotheosis of bureaucracy, casts an interesting light upon the priorities of educational administrators.

The period of the school boards, from 1870 to 1903, saw some interesting developments in the position and work of teachers. Appointment by a school board gave a teacher a certain semi-official status, particularly if he served with one of the large city boards. Rates of pay rose rapidly for the more successful teachers, and, for the first time, a career structure and a stratification appeared in the profession. First there was the building of very large schools in urban centres. These required head-teachers of administrative ability as well as teaching skill, and such men acquired a position very different from that of the head of a small rural school. Second was the appearance of the qualified assistant. Such people were virtually unheard of in the 1850s. It was taken for granted that a qualified teacher would take his own school immediately upon finishing his apprenticeship. By the 1870s the large school boards found it worthwhile to allow for qualified assistants in drawing up their pay scales, and by the 1880s provision was being made for promotion within the grade of assistant, it no longer being assumed that every teacher would finish his career as a head-teacher. At the same time increments were introduced, although these were not, at first, automatic; they became so in the more liberal boards during the 1890s.

The third factor making for stratification was the increasing standard of work done in senior schools. Assistants in higher grade schools regularly received higher pay, but as ordinary elementary schools began to attempt recognizably secondary work, there was a demand for suitably qualified teachers. At the same time teachers began to see that extra qualifications were a way to promotion. The result was that teachers began to take external qualifications. The London matriculation was very popular among teachers; some took the intermediate examination, and a few particularly determined individuals achieved external degrees – fourteen graduates were employed by the Nottingham School Board in 1902. Teachers with additional qualifications, or who were employed on advanced work could expect extra pay as well as accelerated promotion; some boards had a regular scale of bonuses for recognized qualifications.

There were two interesting features of the pay structure for teachers in the school board period. The first of these, which has been briefly noticed before, was the great discrepancy between different boards; there was nothing remotely resembling a national scale. The difference was most marked between urban and rural schools; urban boards habitually paid substantially higher salaries, but there were distinct variations between similarly placed boards. London teachers received high money wages, but the cost of living probably lowered their real value. The rates at Nottingham were higher than those in Sheffield or Derby, but very similar to those in Birmingham, except that senior teachers did better at Nottingham. A teacher who was prepared to move had ample opportunity to improve his situation, and there is evidence that many teachers took advantage of this. Quite a small village school in the East Riding appointed consecutive teachers from King's Lynn, London and Bristol.

The second feature which calls for attention was the distinction between the pay of heads and assistant teachers. The head of a board school was well paid by the standards of the day. If he was head of a higher grade school his income would be £350–£400, while the head of quite a modest school of 300 to 400 children would be paid £250. In either case he would earn twice as much as his senior assistant and three times as much as the ordinary qualified teacher. This had an adverse effect on recruitment, particularly since, as schools tended to become larger and fewer, there was less chance of promotion to a headship. H. B. Philpott, who wrote an interesting contemporary account of the London School Board, pointed out that there was distinct difficulty in obtaining men of the right quality as teachers: 'It is somewhat remarkable that the women teachers of the board – speaking quite generally – seem to be people of more natural refinement than the men. And the explanation, no doubt, is the simple one that the calling of the School Board teacher is, from the pecuniary point of view, a poor one for men, though a good one for women.' The position was really quite serious and there was a distinct possibility of elementary teaching becoming a female profession. All boards were finding difficulty in recruiting male pupil-teachers; in 1902 Nottingham apprenticed twenty-three girls and one boy, but even this was better than Birmingham where no boy was apprenticed for ten years after 1893.

A feature of the school board period was friction between teachers and administrators. To some extent this was due to the increasing professional awareness of the teachers, but it also reflects the fact, so familiar to teachers ever since, that the administrators were totally out of touch with the school situation, and frequently showed a complete lack of interest in the problems and interests of teachers. Few members of school boards had any professional experience of schools, and even fewer had direct knowledge of elementary schools. The clerks of school boards, who occupied in larger boards a position analogous to the director of education, were generally legally qualified or had business experience. Even inspectors and advisers were rarely ex-elementary school teachers; there was a prejudice against the appointment of such men to even the local inspectorate on the grounds that their academic background was suspect, and that their outlook upon education was limited. In essence the problem, then as now, was that educational policy making was in the hands of amateurs, who rarely saw the need for knowledge of educational problems, and were frequently not even aware that specifically educational problems existed.

The small one-school boards were often notorious for their exploitation of teachers, and there were occasions when HMIs found it necessary to intercede on the teachers' behalf. Most evidence, however, comes from the larger boards where the teachers, being more numerous, were able to resist; in the small boards the single teacher was almost completely helpless against the board. Dissatisfaction among teachers was very widespread. In Birmingham it reached the point where the teachers ran their own candidate in the school board elections of 1894; he topped the poll with a large majority. The particular grievance there was of over-interference by the board officials in the schools' work.

The chief inspector visited each department twice a year, the inspector of registers once a month, his assistants once a month each, the inspector of singing twice a year, sometimes more, the drill inspector, who did teach when he came, and was therefore welcome, called twice, the hand and eye training super-intendant looked in, the inspector of needlework called twice; the inspector of schools and his two assistants took at least a week over their work and sometimes a fortnight, making at the lowest estimate ten visits, then there was the grand parade before HMI. Altogether there were 49 visits during the year.

In Bradford there were continual complaints that teachers were autocratically treated by the board officials, and there was at least one court case between the board and a head-teacher over wrongful dismissal – which was won by the teacher. The vice-president of the West Yorkshire Union of Elementary Teachers began a speech there with the words, 'I am aware that I am speaking in a town where teachers are ground under a hard servitude'. The situation was similar in London where there was chronic discontent. A contemporary observer noted,

The School Board, or perhaps it would be more correct to say certain powerful members of the Board, have maintained a peculiarly unsympathetic and suspicious attitude towards the teachers, which has resulted in much irritation. And thus it happens that, while on public grounds teachers are generally deploring the destruction of the London School Board, many of them are rejoicing privately in the hope that the change may give them a more sympathetic and tactful body of employers.

In general, however, the school board period saw a rapid rise in the status of the teacher. Pay rose rapidly, and there were, for the first time, opportunities of promotion for men and women who were willing to improve upon their basic qualifications. The head of a large board school enjoyed a salary and status far in advance of any previous elementary teacher. In some boards there were openings for teachers in administra-tion and inspection; the Nottingham board – admittedly an exception – appointed all its senior officers from the ranks of teachers. An important reason for the increased status of teachers was the rapid rise in the standard of work they were called upon to do. There was even some blurring of the boundaries between elementary and secondary education, and it became worthwhile for a few graduates to follow a career in teaching, usually in higher grade schools. Professional organization took great strides in this period; the disputes with school boards were a sign that teachers were conscious of possessing a position which was worth defending and which allowed for development. The teacher had come a long way since the beginning of the century.

The period between 1902 and 1944 saw a consolidation of the position taken up under the school boards. The status of the teacher as a minor functionary was confirmed by his appointment to a local education authority, and there was a much-needed levelling up between rural and urban areas in respect of pay and working conditions. The increase in opportunity for training provided by the new local authority training colleges meant that a far larger proportion of teachers were fully qualified, and the prestige gained from this development was enhanced by the continued rise in the standard of school work, which was underlined by the Hadow reorganization. There were interesting experiments in post-primary education in the twenties and thirties, which made it clear that elementary school teachers were capable of advanced work when required.

The attitude of the new Board of Education, particularly in the Morant era from 1902 to 1911 was curiously ambivalent. One of the most important results of Morant's work was to reestablish the absolute distinction between elementary and secondary education, which had become blurred by the school boards' experiments with higher grade schools. The elementary schools were firmly shut out from secondary education, which was to be the sole function of grammar schools. This was not merely a matter of terminology; secondary school masters were paid on a different scale and enjoyed a far higher social status than elementary school teachers.

On the other hand Morant did much to liberalize the attitude of the Board of Education and of local authorities towards elementary schools and their teachers. The Revised Code and the system of 'payment by results' were based upon the assumption that teaching could not be safely left to teachers who had to be supervized minutely by inspectors. This was an assumption which school boards were only too eager to adopt, and the local education authorities generally followed suit. The results, in terms of over-inspection and a general attitude of suspicion and niggling criticism, have been discussed in the previous section. It would be too optimistic a view to maintain that this attitude has been entirely worked out at the present time, but Morant must be given the credit for taking a different line at the board, and thus establishing a happy precedent. In the *Code for Public Elementary Schools* of 1904 and the *Handbook of Suggestions* of the following year, an attitude was taken up towards the teacher which was entirely opposed to that of the old code. The title alone of the *Handbook* suggested a less authoritarian approach, and, as was mentioned in chapter 4, the preface asked that 'each teacher shall think for himself, and work out for himself such methods of teaching as may use his powers to their best advantage and be best suited to the particular needs and conditions of the schools'.

This changed attitude took notice of the important alteration in the organization of schools which had come about due to the appearance of the large school with many qualified teachers. The detailed supervision which the old style head-teacher had exercised over his pupil-teachers was no longer possible, or necessary. A move had to be made towards the concept of the assistant teacher as a competent person who enjoyed a substantial measure of autonomy in his work in the classroom. *The Handbook of Suggestions* was of major significance in helping to create an atmosphere in which this move could take place, but it is curious how the old attitude has persisted, and (even up to the 1960s) one of the most conspicuous differences between the grammar schools and other second-ary schools has been in the relatively close supervision exercised by the secondary modern school headmaster over the activities of his staff. In this respect it is dubious whether the ideal laid down by Morant in 1905 has ever been achieved, but the *Handbook of Suggestions* remains a major landmark in the process by which the control of the teacher over what he taught and how he taught it was steadily increased. It is only within the last few years that this process has been reversed.

Since 1944 there have been major developments in the status of the teacher. These developments are still in progress and it is far from certain what their final outcome will be. In essence, the teacher's position as a respectable tradesman, with a recognizable skill, was established by the beginning of the century; what has been in question since the Second World War is the teacher's claim to be a member of a profession.

Some very definite advances have been made. The divided pay scale has been abandoned, and teachers are now paid on the same basic scale as schoolmasters. This has helped to blur the distinction between the two groups, at least in the minds of laymen – and it is the attitude of laymen which, in the last resort, determines the status of an occupational group. This blurring has been increased by the continued rise in the standard of work done in the schools, characterized by the ventures of secondary modern schools into the examination field. The rather embarrassing success of secondary modern schools with 11+ 'failures', has raised some questions about the relative efficiency of teaching in modern and grammar schools. These questions have been played down recently since the Conservative party, which is the political group traditionally interested in cost-efficiency in education, has got itself into the position of having to defend the grammar schools. Nevertheless the fact remains that the descendants of the elementary schools have been poaching in a field which has traditionally been the preserve of the 'schoolmaster'.

Another confusing factor has been the introduction of comprehensive schools. The social division between the grammar school and modern school staffs, which was viable so long as most grammar schools retained a measure of independence, became increasingly artificial after 1944 when the great majority of these schools fell in to the LEA so that the staffs of all schools were paid at the same rate by the same employer. It became even more artificial when comprehensive schools recruited staff from both sides of the barrier, who had to teach the same children in the same building. To the outsider at least the division became meaningless.

One of the most obvious criteria for drawing the distinction between 'schoolmaster' and 'teacher' lay in the length and type of training followed by each. The schoolmaster was a graduate, untrained but educated. The teacher was a non-graduate, trained, but hardly thought of as an educated man. The schoolmaster spent three years over his degree, possibly more; the teacher's training occupied two years, and, until well into the present century, many teachers had no college training at all.

Since 1944, two developments have tended to close this gap. The prejudice against professional training, still very strong in the public schools, has weakened very much in the grammar schools, and it is becoming the normal thing for a graduate to train before beginning to teach. Indeed, training is about to be made a requirement for all new teachers, graduate or otherwise. An interesting recent development has been the establishment of post-graduate training courses in colleges of education, so that graduate and non-graduate training is being carried out in the same institutions. The suggestion is being canvassed that we should follow the Scottish plan of having all initial training done in colleges of education, and, although there is a long way to go before this change can be effected, the fact that such a suggestion can be entertained illustrates the way in which the gap between universities and colleges has closed in the last generation.

The opposite side to this is that the academic level of the work done in the colleges has been raised. The lengthening of the course from two to three years for entrants in 1960 and afterwards, and the change in name from 'Training Colleges' to 'Colleges of Education', suggest a more ambitious approach to their task. Voices have been raised in complaint about making the courses over-theoretical and over-academic; it has been remarked previously that there has always been opposition to raising the educational level of the teachers of the lower orders too high. It is perhaps fair to ask why no-one ever criticizes the public schools for appointing men of high academic calibre. But whatever the rights or wrongs of the case, the work of students in colleges of education has risen sharply in academic standard, and this has been recognized by the introduction of the bachelor of education degree.

The problem of drawing a clear line between 'schoolmaster' and 'teacher' has, therefore become complicated. Graduates take a professional training and teach in secondary modern or primary schools; students from colleges of education graduate – in education, admittedly, but they graduate nevertheless. The staffs of comprehensive schools are drawn from both camps. The distinction is not dead but the situation is confused, and in the confusion the teacher has gained while the schoolmaster has lost.

This does not mean that the teacher's position is an easy one; in some ways it is in fact more difficult now than ever before. There was a time when the population could be divided with some confidence into the learned and the unlearned. The possession of learning carried privileges, and a very little learning was required to qualify. A man who could read a Latin verse was exempt from the death penalty for many offences until 1827, but for long after this date the ability to read, either in Latin or English was not very widely spread. It was the first great task of the board schools to establish basic literacy among the mass of working population, and until the end of the nineteenth century the teacher did not require much more than the ability to read and write fluently to pass for a man of parts. The success of the board schools in spreading literacy, and the great expansion of secondary education in the twentieth century raised two serious problems for the teacher. Education has become a topic of national importance, and one which is discussed knowledgeably by people who have been exposed to it for ten years or more. Parents and other interested parties, whose own educational standards have risen sharply, expect teachers to be able to discuss educational questions at a depth which they were never expected to reach before. The teacher is open to criticism by parents, governors, journalists, and some of the critics are uncomfortably well informed.

It is against this background that the teachers' present claims to professional status have to be set. Absolutely the standards of training and competence of teachers have increased and are increasing; it is more doubtful whether their standards are increasing relative to the rapidly rising educational standards of the general population. In the land of the blind the one-eyed man is king; where the population is illiterate a little learning goes a long way. Teachers are now faced by the consequences of their own success in solving the problem of illiteracy, and one of these is the necessity of forcing up their own standards of education and training to parallel the rising standards of their present and former pupils.

CHAPTER 7

SECONDARY EDUCATION

In thinking about secondary education in Britain at any period before 1944 it is important to avoid a common and understandable error. At the present time we are accustomed to look upon education, for all social classes, as a single process which is divided for various reasons into three stages – primary, secondary and tertiary. The word 'tertiary' has only recently gained fairly general acceptance, but a stage of 'further' or 'higher' education has been recognized for far longer than the name has been used. We assume that all pupils, except perhaps those suffering from some gross handicap, will go through the primary stage and on to the secondary stage, with a break at about eleven years – or rather older for those in the independent sector. An increasing proportion remain for the tertiary section, admission to the more desirable forms of tertiary education being controlled by examination success. The essence of the system is that one stage arises from and depends upon the previous stage, and this is why we use the terms 'secondary' and 'tertiary'.

Until the very end of the nineteenth century there was absolutely no idea of continuity between primary and secondary schools in the modern sense; in fact the word 'primary' was not used, and 'secondary' had a very different meaning from modern usage. The assumption was that the great bulk of the population had no use for secondary education – however it might be defined, and would be unable to afford it even if they desired it. For these people there were 'elementary' schools, provided by a combination of charity with some public assistance, and giving a basic education in the three 'Rs' with a strong moral content. For working men who had some social pretensions there were cheap private schools, of varying efficiency, but enjoying rather more prestige than the elementary schools at a time when self-help was one of the cardinal virtues. It was for this class that the National and British Societies provided schools and for whom the Forster Act of 1870 was passed.

Completely separate from this system were the schools for the children of those parents who were prepared to lay out a substantial sum on education. It is difficult to draw any very exact line between the two classes, although everybody was quite clear at the time that the line existed, and it was the great aim of private school teachers, for example, to rise from the lower class of 'common day schools' into the ranks of 'writing schools', which were allowed to be at the lower end of the upper class. In 1870 the dividing line was taken to lie at a fee of 9*d.* per week; schools charging less than this were considered to be available to the poor, and an examination of the private schools of the day suggests that this division corresponded to a social fact. Applying a rather similar criterion the census of 1851 estimated that 600,000 children were to be found above the line. When people spoke of secondary schools in the nineteenth century they were thinking of the education of these children; the distinction between elementary and secondary education was quite avowedly social, since it was assumed that only the children of the middle and upper classes could or would benefit from education above the rudiments. The main theme of this chapter is the move from this rigid social stratification, to the acceptance of the 'educational ladder' and then to the ideal of 'secondary education for all'. Attention will be concentrated upon the introduction and development of secondary education for 'the poor', but it will be necessary first of all to glance at developments in 'secondary' education in the nineteenth-century sense, since important changes in attitudes and methods occurred in the early and middle nineteenth century, before the idea of widening its social scope gathered any force.

Children of the middle and upper classes gained their education in one of three ways, or sometimes in a combination of two of them. The method which has attracted most attention from historians, although not numerically the most important was by attendance at the public or endowed grammar schools. Public and grammar schools so dominate the educational scene today that it is a natural mistake to assume that they have always done so; but it is a mistake nevertheless. At the beginning of the nineteenth century these schools had reached the lowest point of their fortunes. The public schools were described in 1810 as 'a system of premature debauchery that only prevents men from being corrupted by the world, by corrupting them before their entry into the world'. Their academic standards were low, their curriculum was limited and archaic, they were grossly understaffed and their moral standards were so low – as the quotation suggests – that thoughtful parents hesitated to send their children there in spite of the social prestige which they still enjoyed. If anything the grammar schools had sunk further. They were saved from the moral collapse of the public schools by the fact that most of them were day schools, but their academic standards had fallen and also their numbers; not a few ceased to function altogether, and many others were merely socially acceptable elementary schools which had given up any claim to academic distinction. Attempts to reform their curricula to permit the teaching of modern subjects were crippled by a legal judgment of 1805 which made it virtually impossible to alter the curriculum as laid down by the founder. This meant that such schools were forced to continue with the Classics whether or not a demand existed, and it was not until 1840 that an act of Parliament allowed governors to make suitable amendments to trust deeds.

Under the circumstances it is not surprising that few children attended the public and grammar schools; in 1851, when conditions, especially in the public schools, had improved considerably, the absolute maximum number of children (nearly all boys) attending such schools was thought to be 50,000.

A curious fact to people used to the modern system is that about 50,000 children were taught at home by tutors and governesses. This was the customary way for a member of the aristocracy to receive his education, as had always been the case. Such children were taught when young by governesses and later by tutors, who were resident. It was an expensive business to keep a full-time tutor, who would be expected to be a graduate capable of preparing a boy for university, but in a great household the post might be combined with that of chaplain, or a young clergyman could be found who would take a post as tutor while waiting for presentation to a benefice. Governesses were cheaper and were employed by many families of quite moderate means to prepare little boys for school or for tutors, and to be responsible for the education of the daughters of the house, since there was still much doubt about the advisability of sending girls out to school. Cheaper still were visiting tutors and governesses. Where there were girls to be taught it was common practice to have a governess in general charge and to employ tutors to provide specialist teaching. Day governesses were looked down upon by their resident colleagues, but quite respectable and successful private school teachers regularly had a private practice, visiting local households to teach the girls mathematics, music, painting, languages and so on. If contemporary fiction is to be relied upon this could be a dangerous practice, since a stock situation for novelists was for the heiress to elope with a visiting tutor; newspaper reports show that such novels had a basis in fact.

Teaching by private tutors was surprisingly common in the nineteenth century even among families in quite modest circumstances. In Manchester in 1851 many of the children who were privately taught came from homes with a rateable value of about £18, which put them in the class of small businessmen, managers or substantial shop-keepers. But by far the most common source of education for the middle and upper classes was the private school. About half a million children of secondary school age were attending private schools in 1851, ten times as many as at public and grammar schools. It was not until the second half of the century that a serious and general attempt was made to put the public and grammar schools in order, and not until after about 1880 that they began to seriously rival private schools and tutors in public esteem. The next topic for consideration is the reason for the revival of what may be called 'public' secondary education, and this is of particular significance since it is from this time that the public and grammar schools began to acquire their present position.

From the very beginning of the nineteenth century there was an increasing demand for efficient secondary education. The rapid increase in the number of private schools at this period is evidence of this demand, and the proprietors of these schools were very much aware of the reasons for the flourishing state of their business. They set out to fill the gap left by the decline of the public and grammar schools by offering a modern curriculum and close personal supervision of the morals and behaviour of the boys, particularly the boarders. But even while the private schools were flourishing the public schools began to reform themselves, followed by some at least of the grammar schools.

There were various reasons for this development, several of which are treated either in chapter 2 or chapter 5 and will only be referred to here. One of the most important was the realization that the classical curriculum was out of date. There were two possible responses to this, and both were tried. One was to introduce new subjects, and most of the subjects now familiar in secondary schools began to appear at this time as school subjects, private schools usually leading the way, and being copied by 'public' schools. The difficulty here was that no-one really knew how to teach these new subjects; as the headmaster of Winchester remarked, 'I wish we could teach more history, but as to teaching it in set lessons, I would not know how to do it.' In expressing this view Dr Moberley was perhaps wiser than his contemporaries who rushed into history teaching where he feared to tread.

The other response was to so alter the teaching of Classics that it became a relevant and useful study, and this was the approach adopted by Thomas Arnold at Rugby, and by many of the other mid-nineteenth-century headmasters who brought about the revival of the public schools. A result of this was that the classical curriculum gained a new life, and was perhaps more firmly entrenched in the public schools and their imitators at the end of the nineteenth century than it was at the beginning.

The demand for a modern curriculum received some support from fear of industrial and commercial rivalry by Germany, France and other overseas competitors, but this was not very important before the Great Exhibition of 1851, and throughout the nineteenth century there was curiously little public call for technical training by public and grammar schools. The rise of the higher grade schools, which will be discussed a little later in the chapter, was certainly fostered by the felt need for better trained men of the technician grade, but with certain notable exceptions, like Prince Albert or Lyon Playfair – both educated at least partly in Germany – the English were never really convinced of the need for scientific or technological training for managers and directors. What such men needed, it was felt, was a good liberal education, and with their minds so prepared they would be able to acquire any technical knowledge which they might need. On the other hand there was an increasing demand for young men to serve as army officers or administrators in the rapidly expanding Empire, and for them, too, a liberal education was felt to be a necessity, the necessary military or administrative knowledge being added 'on the job' afterwards. Secondary schools were therefore in a seller's market, but since many of the parents were businessmen or men of affairs, they were inclined to expect an efficient education in return for the very high fees charged by the public schools; and the flourishing private schools provided formidable competition.

The demand for efficiency was not confined to the intellectual field. The end of the eighteenth and the early nineteenth centuries was a period of very marked revival in moral and religious standards, Methodism being one aspect of this revival. The eighteenth century had been prepared to tolerate a very low moral tone and a total lack of supervision by teachers, but in the age of Wilberforce and Shaftesbury this could not continue. The popularity of private schools rested on their insistence on a close, often oppressive, watch on the children's behaviour, and headmasters were quick to realize that in this matter the public schools would have to reform. In fact many of the headmasters were themselves men of strong moral convictions, eager to put a stop to the anarchy and brutal bullying which were characteristic of the eighteenth-century boarding school, but their position was undoubtedly strengthened by the support of parents and of public opinion in general.

It may be that a contributing factor to the moral revival of the public schools was a change in their clientele. It was in the nineteenth century that it became common for parents of the upper middle class – professional men, substantial businessmen and industrialists – to send their children to these schools. Social mobility was increasing but such men felt some insecurity, and no doubt hoped to establish at least their sons' position by sending them to the schools patronized by the nobility and gentry. But they were often men of an evangelical character, and looked for a high moral tone in their children's schools.

There were two separate but related developments in the public school field. On the one hand the existing schools were reformed, and on the other, new schools were established. Thomas Arnold, of Rugby, has achieved fame as the paradigm case of a reforming headmaster, and it is certain that he was immensely influential, both directly and through the work of men who were influenced by him, but there were many other headmasters who reorganized their schools and experimented with curricula and organization. They improved the moral tone of the schools, and made an important contribution to educational practice by breaking down the belief in the inevitable hostility between teacher and pupil; important experiments were made in allowing responsibility to senior pupils. Boarding arrangements were made more civilized, and a tradition established that teachers were responsible for the moral and social development of their pupils as much as for their intellectual development. We have to make a conscious effort to think ourselves into the eighteenth-century frame of mind to realize what an innovation this was, since it has been accepted as an article of faith in British and American schools for a long time now. But this was one of the ideas which were particularly characteristic of the reforms of Thomas Arnold and were publicized by his son, Matthew, and by Thomas Hughes in *Tom Brown's Schooldays*. It is significant that the teacher's responsibility is given a much narrower interpretation on the Continent than in Britain or America, and that welfare and discipline are often considered to come under the aegis of separate, non-academic members of staff.

The work of Arnold and other reforming headmasters raised the old public schools to a position of pre-eminence which they had not enjoyed since the seventeenth century. But the demand for the kind of education which they offered was such that a large number of new schools, was founded. These were set up on a non-profit making basis and were originally known as 'proprietorial' schools, to distinguish them from 'private' schools on the one hand, and the accredited 'public' schools on the other. For many years now, however, they have all been classed as public schools, and this is a convenient usage. Not all these new public schools were absolutely new; enterprising headmasters of old-established grammar schools were sometimes able to elevate their schools into this class – Uppingham and Pocklington are two examples from different parts of the country.

The early 'proprietorial' schools were usually for day pupils, and for that reason were nearly always to be found in the large towns where there was a large population nearby to be tapped. Liverpool Institute, 1825, Liverpool College, 1840, and a number of London schools belong to this period, before the efforts of Arnold and others had made parents less wary of risking their children at boarding schools. But the newly recovered prestige of the public schools led to the establishment of a number of new boarding schools in the 1830s, and the following years. Cheltenham, Marlborough, Wellington, Hailebury, Lancing and Ardingley are only examples of the substantial number of boarding schools founded in this period. No doubt their popularity was enhanced by the spread of the railways, which made travelling to and from school less of an adventure.

From our point of view there is no need to distinguish between the old and new public schools since the new schools were quite avowedly founded upon the model of the old. There were one or two exceptions, but in general they shared certain characteristics which are of major importance to this study, since it was upon the model of these schools that the revived grammar schools were organized in the last quarter of the nineteenth century and the first years of the twentieth. It is worthwhile to look critically at these characteristics since they have been absorbed into the 'grammar school tradition' of which so much is heard in controversies about comprehensive schools, and it is always a useful exercise to study the origins of a tradition as a guide to its contemporary relevance.

The first feature which stands out is that the public schools were strongly religious in tone. To Arnold the chapel was the centre of the school, and it was by his addresses there that he hoped to exercise influence upon the school as a whole. This, of course, is very understandable since Arnold, like the great majority of nineteenth-century headmasters, was a clergyman. Furthermore, as has been previously noted, much of the drive for reform of the public schools came from the religious revival, of which Arnold was himself an important advocate. This is a part of the public school practice which has been taken over almost unchanged by the grammar school and by the secondary modern school. The present-day headmaster is rarely in orders, and the chapel has been replaced by the school hall, but the daily assembly is still a religious service, it is the only occasion when the whole school is gathered as a unit and it is the occasion for reproof and exhortation by the headmaster. This is one of those customs which is so entrenched that it has come to be accepted as an obvious part of any school routine. It is an effort to think it away. But the fact remains that the school assembly as we know it was an invention of the reforming public school headmasters of the nineteenth century.

Another invention which has become a permanency is the sixth form. Senior pupils, obviously, there have always been, but until Arnold's day they were merely the ringleaders of the pupils against the staff, and in the vicious bullying which was one of the worst features of eighteenth-century schools. It was Arnold who turned these boys into the pillars of the school by giving them an enormous degree of responsibility for the discipline of the school and the running of its social and athletic life. This innovation was developed by his followers so that in many schools the position of head boy or captain of the eleven was far more honourable and carried more power than that of assistant master. Day schools have not taken this tradition over in its most extreme form; they are not such enclosed institutions as boarding schools and boys have interests outside the school circle, but the sixth form enjoys substantial privileges and usually has disciplinary powers, though of a limited kind. Secondary modern and primary schools have copied the sixth form idea for their senior pupils, although with necessary adjustments to allow for the age of the children concerned.

So far we have been concerned with elements in the public school ethos with which one would not want to disagree. Any educational practice is open to perversion. One has met the headmaster who started an assembly by bellowing 'Shut up and get your minds on God', and there are many more who find assembly a tedious chore and communicate the fact to the school. But the idea that the school should meet as a unit and that the headmaster – presumably a man of experience and character – should use the occasion to impress his personality upon the school has obvious validity. If the headmaster fails to take the opportunity the failure is his, not the system's.

But the secondary school of today has inherited certain features from the reformed nineteenth-century boarding school which, whatever their value in their context, are at least of dubious use when transferred. First among these is the house system. The relevance of this to a boarding school is obvious enough, but it is much less easy to see why it should be adopted in day schools, and, in fact, the house system is rarely very significant in grammar and modern schools, although almost invariably adopted, since it has no sound basis in the communal life of a residential house. The only *raison d'être* of the house system in most schools is to provide an excuse for outbursts of competition, and it is at least arguable that the emphasis on competition in the English educational system is much overdone. One may question whether the spirit of 'my house right or wrong' has anything to do with the critical spirit which is thought to be a feature of education.

This reflection raises the question of the second rather dubious legacy of the public schools to English secondary education – organized games. Again these have an obvious justification in a boarding school, but are less immediately relevant to the day school. In the event they have been used as occasions for stirring up a xenophobic form of house spirit which is more characteristic of the professional football ground than the school playing field. In justice to grammar and modern schools it must be said that this process has not generally been allowed to go so far as it did in the public schools where athleticism became a cult, there was an unhealthy tendency to hero worship successful athletes, and where success on the field was given far more prominence than intellectual achievement. Perhaps the strongly vocational interest in academic success which is such a feature of the grammar school has exerted a useful influence in moderating the excesses of the public schools in this direction.

There was one other feature of the reformed public schools which was important in its day, and which has been transmitted to the grammar schools. For reasons which are sufficiently obvious it has not been passed on to secondary modern schools. This was the ideal of education for leadership. One of the major factors causing the revival of the public schools was the call for men who had been educated as officers, administrators, judges and so on, so that it is not surprising that these schools laid emphasis upon the education of an elite. In the social framework of the time it would have been very surprising if they had not done so, since class consciousness was still very strong – perhaps the stronger since the well understood class structure of the eighteenth century was being undermined by social changes associated with the industrial revolution. It is interesting, in this connection, to observe that the tripartite system of secondary education, so popular among planners of the 1930s and 1940s, was already being actively canvassed a hundred years earlier. The Woodard schools, Church of England boarding schools established from the 1840s under the aegis of Canon Woodard, were specifically planned for three different grades of middle-class children. The three grades were expected to leave school at different ages – about fourteen, sixteen and eighteen years, and it was supposed that they would correspond to the lower-middle, middle-middle and upper-middle classes respectively, fees being fixed accordingly. The chief determining factor in the leaving age, apart from the parental income, would be the proposed career of the boy, and it was taken for granted that this would be largely settled by the parents' profession.

About the middle of the nineteenth century the idea arose of providing secondary education for selected members of the working class. This, of course, was not entirely a new idea. Many grammar schools had originally been founded, at least partly, in order to provide an education for poor scholars who could proceed to university, and then into the Church, and in Tudor and Stuart times this 'educational ladder' had existed and been used. But by the early nineteenth century these schools had either become moribund or had been deliberately rendered socially exclusive by enterprising headmasters who wished to raise them to the rank of public schools. For a number of reasons the idea of the 'educational ladder' was revived in mid-nineteenth century, and during the next half-century it attained general acceptance.

Support for this extension of secondary education came from several directions. Politicians and industrialists were moved to propose secondary education for the working class largely because of the previously noted motive that they were afraid of the competition of countries such as Germany, France and the United States, whose industrial success they attributed, in part at least, to their efficient secondary and technical education. For the most part these men hoped to improve the quality of the intermediate grades of industrial employment – technicians, clerks, foremen – for whom there was absolutely no form of education available, apart from the private 'writing schools', which generally concentrated upon commercial training. Technical education hardly existed at all. It was at this period, however, that it first began to be argued that not to provide an efficient education for the working class resulted in a serious wastage of talent, since many potential inventors might exist whose capacities were masked by their lack of education. A writer of 1844 stated the case as follows: 'I want every workshop in the country to be filled with experimenters, and especially with men, who, from reading and thinking shall have learned how experimenting may be done with advantage. If such were the case – if it were as much so as it might easily be – who can doubt that an incredible multitude and variety of inventions and improvements in the arts would spring up in every direction . . .'

From within the ranks of the working class support for the extension of secondary education sprang from two sources. In the second half of the nineteenth century the lead in working-class political and social movements was taken by the 'moral force' advocates who drew strength from the failure of 'physical force' Chartism, and from the generally less embittered state of industrial relations which followed the troubles of the 1830s and 1840s. Education was a major factor in the 'moral force' programme which naturally favoured any extension of educational opportunity to members of the working class. In addition to this general attitude of benevolence there was a specific factor of some importance. In this period there was a rapid increase in the scale of working-class organization. Trades unions became larger and there was a movement towards political organization upon a national scale, and independent of the existing political parties. Working-class representatives, under various labels, appeared as candidates, sometimes successfully, in local government and school board elections, and eventually in parliamentary elections. It was obviously an advantage to such men if they could obtain a secondary education, which allowed them to meet their opponents in debate upon equal terms.

It is, in fact, very doubtful how far the educational ladder, as interpreted at this period, answered the political requirements of the working class. A child of working-class origin who, by one means or another was selected for secondary education, faced a problem which is, of course, very familiar today. The school he attended was overwhelmingly supported by middle-class families, and its ethos was firmly middle class. Unless a scholarship boy wished to aggravate the prejudice against himself which already existed, he had to absorb this ethos as quickly as possible, and the more successful he was in this process, the more he isolated himself from his social origins. Rather than a leader of the working class, he became a member of the middle class by virtue of his secondary education. The Labour movement was not slow to realize that the educational ladder, however advantageous to individual members of the working class, was not in the political interests of the class as a whole, and developed a hostility towards grammar schools which has been very marked since the Second World War. The enthusiasm of the Conservative party for grammar schools no doubt springs from the same line of reasoning.

Projects to provide secondary education for the working class received support from the very strong nineteenth-century belief in the virtues of self-improvement. There was a great admiration for the self-made man, and men who rose from obscurity to eminence were held up as models for emulation in books, lectures and sermons. Samuel Smiles was probably the best known exponent of this point of view in *The Lives of the Great Engineers*, and particularly in the enormously popular *Self Help*, but he had numerous colleagues and imitators, like the lecturer who addressed working men's associations in a large industrial town upon, 'The Life and Character of John Kitto, who by his perseverance and piety raised himself from a poor, deaf workhouse lad to the honourable position of doctor of divinity'. Under the circumstances it obviously made sense to provide educational facilities by which talented and ambitious working-class children could rise in the world. At this time there was no notion of giving secondary education to the whole working class, but only to individual members, who, as was remarked previously, achieved middle-class status by virtue of their educational qualifications. This was the beginning, in modern times at least, of the idea of the 'meritocracy'.

There were other factors leading to an expansion of secondary education in this period. The working class was not the only under-privileged group; women also fell into this category. Throughout the second half of the nineteenth century there was a movement which progressively gathered strength, to remove the disabilities, political, legal and social, under which women laboured. There were parallels between the working-class movements of the time and the movement for the emancipation of women. For example there was the same division into those who favoured constitutional methods of protest and agitation, and those who advocated a more drastic, even violent, policy, and, as with the Labour movement, there was a tendency in the early years of this century for the 'physical force' wing to gain the upper hand, particularly in the period immediately before the First World War. Another similarity was that the leaders of the campaign for women's emancipation laid great emphasis on the necessity for the education of women to be improved, and in particular for rational secondary education to be available to girls as a necessary preparation for their proceeding to higher education.

A final factor was a demand from within the elementary school system for more advanced courses to be provided. This was perhaps the most important factor of all; certainly it led to the provision of the first recognizably secondary schools which were readily available to the working class. As the battle to lengthen the school life of working-class children was won in the late 1870s and 1880s there arose, quite spontaneously, a demand for education at a level above that hitherto provided in elementary schools. This demand became increasingly powerful throughout the school board period, and the larger boards produced some interesting answers in their efforts to meet it. What had happened was that the very success of the elementary schools had rendered the existing concept of elementary education obsolete, and this in turn put into question the distinction between elementary and secondary education, a point which will be developed in the next section. A very similar development within recent years has been the movement of secondary modern schools into the external examination field, which has been considered the preserve of grammar schools. The fairly clear dividing line between the grammar schools, where pupils took GCE, and modern schools, where they did not, has been blurred, and there is very apparent confusion about the precise function within a system of education of either type of school.

These various factors led to a number of developments in the field of what may generally be called secondary education in the last quarter of the nineteenth century. The most widespread of these was the widening of the curriculum of the ordinary elementary school which has already been referred to in chapter 4. It is proper to refer to this change as relating to secondary education since it involved the introduction of certain subjects, cookery, science, wood and metal work for example, specifically for older pupils of Standard IV or V and above. Here was a rudimentary division of education into 'primary' and 'secondary' sectors in the modern sense, although the word 'secondary' was normally reserved to describe work done in a grammar school. This was an anticipation of the phenomenon which impressed the Hadow Committee and caused it to recommend a break in a pupil's education to allow a recognizable distinction to be made between elementary and senior work, and it will be noticed that it was the beginning of the process by which the distinction between elementary and secondary schools ceased to be one of social class and became merely a question of the pupil's age. Of course the extent to which the curriculum of the elementary school was expanded varied immensely between different school boards, as a rule urban boards being more adventurous than rural, largely because they were dealing with greater numbers of children and could afford some rudimentary specialization among their teachers.

In some areas, at least, there was a reaction against this widening of the curriculum when the Local Education Authorities took over from the school boards in 1903. Thus, as early as 1905, the Annual Report of the Nottingham Education Committee contained a clear statement of an intention not merely to prevent further expansion of the curriculum, but to reduce its scope: 'The Committee is strongly of the opinion that the most skillful and successful teachers are those who limit themselves, in the case of children who leave school as soon as is permitted by law, to teaching intelligently and well the rudiments of reading, writing and arithmetic, with special reference to the actual requirements of every-day life.' This was the first shot in a campaign which continued until the First World War, and after complaining for many years that the curriculum of elementary schools was too extensive, the Education Committee issued a circular to schools in February 1914 which requested head-teachers 'to make spelling, writing and arithmetic, by formal lessons, fundamental subjects of instruction; and to introduce additional subjects only so far as they can be taught without interfering with the intelligent and thorough grounding of scholars in these essential subjects'. The committee went on to state that, 'in assessing the character of the work in any school, special importance will be attached to the manner in which such a school has succeeded in teaching the fundamental subjects'.

Here is a prime example of the alternation in English education of periods of experiment when 'progressive' views are in favour with periods when the climate of opinion has swung towards more cautious 'reactionary' policies. An earlier example of the same process was the cutting-off of the experiments of the Kay-Shuttleworth era by the Revised Code of 1862, and in the late 1960s the 'progressive' and expansionist ideas which have generally been in favour since the Second World War have been strongly challenged, notably but not exclusively by thinkers of the 'Black Paper' school.

In large urban school boards higher grade schools were established by bringing together in central institutions those older pupils from the town's elementary schools who wished to pursue more advanced studies. The most interesting feature of the higher grade schools was their attempt to produce a vocational kind of secondary education. Often, but by no means always, their curricula were biased rather heavily towards the vocational side, a bias which was increased by their dependence upon the grants of the Science and Art Department. Generally these schools concentrated upon science and technical subjects, but there were also commercial schools, and in the 1890s some schools were entering their pupils for leaving examinations – the College of Preceptors examination, Oxford and Cambridge local examinations or London matriculation. The commercial schools were originally intended mainly for boys, but it was not long before girls came to preponderate on this type of course. There were school boards where the educational ladder was extended to reach higher education and it was possible for pupils to pass either directly from higher grade school to the local university college, or to go from higher grade school to a grammar school and then on to university. Such pupils were exceptional, but it was not particularly unusual for higher grade school pupils to win their way to university; between 1892 and 1898 at least eleven pupils from Nottingham schools did so.

Higher grade schools were never very numerous. They only existed in large towns and only a few of these produced anything like a system of higher grade schooling. They received very little encouragement from the Education Department, which is natural enough since their legality was extremely dubious,[1] and they did not exist for long enough to reach their full development. They were cut off by the events leading up to the 1902 Education Act when they were still at an experimental stage, and it is natural to wonder if they might eventually have found an answer to the still existing problem of the balance between 'vocational' and 'liberal' elements in secondary education.

It was pointed out earlier that the developments of the last quarter of the nineteenth century had rendered obsolete the existing concepts of elementary and secondary education and of the relationship between them. Between 1895 and 1910 these concepts were redefined. There was no further wholesale redefinition until 1944, and many of the features of the system established in this period still exist at the present day. In matters like this one must avoid attributing too much to the activities of one man; there were many influences bearing upon the development of English education about the time of the 1902 Act, but the fact remains that the principal influence at work was that of Sir Robert Morant. The results of this redefinition may be considered as falling under three headings.

First, it reaffirmed the sharp distinction between the elementary and secondary school systems, and completely rejected the notion of a general end-on connection between them. The distinction was based partly upon social considerations – the bulk of the pupils in secondary schools were fee-paying, and therefore from the middle class – and partly upon differences in curricula. Secondary schools followed a curriculum which had a literary and non-vocational bias. The course was built around English, which replaced Latin as the core subject, but it was assumed that Latin would be taken by many pupils, certainly by the more academic ones. By contrast the new higher elementary schools, which were proposed as successors to the higher grade schools were forced to restrict their curricula which was given a strong vocational slant. At the same time they were effectually prevented from entering the field of public examinations by a rule which obliged pupils to leave as soon as they reached fifteen years.

But while the distinction between elementary and secondary schools was confirmed the education ladder was given official recognition, and institutionalized by the 'Free Place' regulations of 1907. These laid down that government grant would only be paid to those secondary schools which made a set proportion, originally one quarter, of their places available to children from elementary schools. This was in effect the

---

[1] The legal status of the higher grade schools and their abolition is admirably treated by E. J. R. Eaglesham in *From School Board to Local Authority* (Routledge and Kegan Paul, 1956).

beginning of the 11+ examination, although certain school boards and local education authorities had previously organized their own selection procedures for higher grade schools and the new municipal grammar schools established following the 1902 Act. It should be noted, however, that the examinations for free places – 'the scholarship' as it came to be called – was at this time a test in ordinary school subjects; it was the development of mental testing techniques in the First World War for the placing of recruits in the armed forces which led to the adoption of standardized tests for secondary school selection. The adoption of the Free Place system led to a rapid increase in the number of elementary school children who found their way to secondary school. In the 1890s the proportion was very small, perhaps 5 or 6 per 1,000; by 1914 56 per 1,000 were doing so. Further the regulations led to secondary education becoming available in areas where no higher grade schools had existed. Very wide differences remained, as they still do, between different parts of the country in the number of places available in secondary schools, and as usual urban areas were generally better catered for than rural, but the process of levelling-up had begun.

The third aspect of this redefinition of secondary education, and this was largely a practical corollary of the first, was that the public school image was imprinted upon the new grammar or secondary schools. This was not a surprising development. At the beginning of the twentieth century there was no grammar school tradition. As has been previously remarked, the old grammar schools, very flourishing in the sixteenth and seventeenth centuries had declined, often to the point of extinction, in the eighteenth and early nineteenth. A paradigm case is that of Queen Elizabeth's Grammar School, Mansfield. When the Taunton Commission investigated this school in the 1860s it found that the headmaster and assistant were both enjoying their salaries, although neither had taken a pupil for some years, and that they had added insult to injury by letting the school-house to a private schoolmaster. Not all schools had sunk to these depths but there was no general recovery until the end of the century when the new interest in secondary education which had inspired the appointment of the Clarendon and Taunton Commissions began to take effect.

Thus nobody had much idea what a modern secondary school or its curriculum should be like, and ideas were taken from various sources. Some were borrowed from private schools, which had been grappling with this problem for many years. The higher grade schools provided a possible model, but this was rejected because of their vocational emphasis which was out of favour. Foreign systems, particularly German, were examined, but the most obvious model was that of the public schools

131

which had been reformed earlier in the century and were in a flourishing state. A particularly powerful reason for the adoption of this model was that the headmasters and staffs of the new and revived secondary schools were largely drawn from the public schools, there being really no alternative source. It was in this way that the house system, the prefect system, the sixth form, the emphasis upon organized games, the cadet force in its various manifestations, found their way into the secondary school. And, of course, later, when the Hadow reorganization was effected the grammar schools formed the model for the new 'senior' and 'secondary modern' schools, which absorbed many of the same ideas.

Another feature of the new secondary schools which was taken over from the public schools was the assumption that pupils would proceed to university or at least the professions on completion of their course, and would, therefore, continue at school for a substantial period in the sixth form. In the majority of schools this assumption never related very closely to the facts of the case, and it is only since the Second World War, and particularly in the last few years, that it could be said that staying on into the sixth form was anything like the general practice. In many schools prior to 1939 there was difficulty in insisting that pupils remained until they took the General School Certificate at fifteen or sixteen years of age. A consequence of this situation was that those pupils who did leave without a substantial period in the sixth form were following a truncated course, which did not meet the requirements of either a 'liberal' or a 'vocational' education.

The expansion of secondary education on the lines laid down by the new definition adopted at the time of the 1902 Act went by fits and starts. For a few years after 1902 progress was rather slow as the new local education authorities got into their stride and groped for an understanding of their functions. In this period the Board of Education played an important part in educating local education authorities in their roles in the provision of secondary education, this being an interesting contrast with the negative attitude of the Education Department at the time of the higher grade school disputes in the 1880s and 1890s. The phase of expansion really began, outside certain large towns, with the Free Place regulations of 1907, and there was a sharp acceleration in progress during the war years, perhaps due as much as anything to the improved economic position of the working class. Thus between 1914 and 1921 the proportion of elementary school children proceeding to secondary school increased from 56 per 1,000 to 97 per 1,000.

Progress was checked by the recurrent economic troubles of the 1920s, but it did not altogether cease, and by the middle 1930s there were about a quarter of a million free or partly free places in secondary schools. One of the consequences of the economies adopted by the government during the slump of 1931 was that 'Free Places' now became 'Special Places', and a sliding scale of fees was introduced, geared to parents' income. The idea of the 'educational ladder' was being put into practice, although there remained great difficulties in the way of working-class children who wished to proceed to secondary and higher education, and a depressing number of offers of free places were turned down, either because of the strain upon a limited budget involved in keeping a child at school beyond the minimum leaving age, or of parental apathy or hostility towards education, or because parents did not wish a child to enter an institution with an ethos very different from their own.

But at the very time when the educational ladder was becoming a reality the attitude of mind from which it sprang was being challenged. The thinking behind the establishment of the ladder was 'elitist' or 'meritocratic' in character. Pupils who possessed particular talent were to be picked out from their fellows and given a special education which would suit them for a career which involved professional skill or responsibility. It was understood that the education of the unselected would be aimed at the production of the 'other ranks' of society while the secondary schools and public schools would produce the officers. At one time or another attempts have been made to insert a middle grade of school – higher elementary, senior or secondary technical – whose function was to provide non-commissioned officers and technicians, but the tripartite system has never taken root and such schools have always been in a minority, although sometimes locally successful.

This was a form of 'contest mobility' in which the prizes went to those who did best at school. Of course in the period under review there was never a condition of genuine contest mobility, since parents with money could always buy a secondary education for their children, and, as has just been observed, there were barriers in the way of a working-class child even if he obtained a free place. These barriers were, in fact, higher than was realized, for at that time rather little attention was given to the influence of a child's home environment upon his ability to benefit from a particular form of education; it was too easily assumed that all problems had been solved when a child had accepted a free place. Nevertheless it was possible to separate the idea of an educational ladder from its more or less accidental inadequacies, which might, at least in principle, be remedied.

The idea was attacked from two directions, and since 1944 the two attacks have been combined to constitute a very serious challenge to the system of selective secondary education which was the logical outcome of the meritocratic attitude. The resulting dispute remains a very live issue today. On the one hand the question was raised whether it was in fact possible to carry out the necessary process of selection with any confidence. From the earliest days selection was carried out at ten or eleven. It is not quite clear whether this was because the minimum school-leaving age was eleven, or whether it was a carry over from the higher grade schools, which had generally taken pupils at that age. However this may be the choice of eleven years as the age of transfer was a historical accident which became sanctified by the Hadow Report. It was fairly asked whether a test at eleven years could be predictive of future success, academic or professional, and this question was given added force in the 1930s as evidence began to be accumulated of the subjectivity and unreliability of current examination techniques. Clearly a meritocracy relies upon merit being recognizable and recognized and cannot function if no efficient test of merit exists. For many years this question was not pressed very hard, partly because the very general acceptance of the idea of the educational ladder did not dispose people to enquire too closely into its working and partly because the introduction of standardized mental tests seemed to offer a method of selection which combined predictive value with objectivity. Although professional psychologists expressed reservations about the uncritical acceptance of the results of these tests in selection much earlier, there was no general swing of opinion against them until the late 1950s, and it is doubtful whether this change of attitude would have occurred even then if the principle of selection had not been undermined from another angle.

It has been mentioned that during the school board period there was a rapid development in the curriculum of ordinary elementary schools, which involved the addition of certain subjects specifically for older pupils, and that this brought with it an embryo division of elementary schools into junior and senior sections. In fact the habit arose of referring to the 'upper standards' and 'lower standards' as distinct entities. It is not clear that the logic of this development was fully appreciated at the time, but there was here an alternative criterion of division between elementary and secondary education, based not upon the social class or the vocational destination of the pupils, but upon their age. If the existing system was based upon the model of a ladder from one level of schooling to another, which only the most successful could scale, the alternative system took the model of a staircase in two flights – primary and secondary – up which all pupils could climb.

Support for the alternative scheme came from two sources. It was favoured by the Labour party, perhaps particularly by the intellectual wing, represented by men like R. H. Tawney, on the grounds that an egalitarian, socialist society could not be brought fully into existence while the educational system was organized upon elitist grounds. Socialists saw education as a means of bringing about the kind of society they favoured. In this, of course, they were merely reviving from a different point of view the recurrent idea of using education as an instrument of social policy, but it is a reflection upon the differing attitudes of the nineteenth and twentieth centuries towards change, that education had hitherto been looked upon as a device for supporting the existing state of affairs; it was now proposed as a means of bringing about radical alterations in the social structure, a proposal which has nowadays become so commonplace as hardly to attract comment. From 1916 the Labour party included in its official policy a programme of 'secondary education for all'. It is probably true to say that there was more enthusiasm for this measure among the intellectual wing of the party than among the bulk of the membership. On achieving power in 1945 the Labour government allowed the very general requirements of the 1944 Act upon secondary education to be underwritten by the ministry in such a way that the selective system became more firmly entrenched than ever, although the method of selection was made to discriminate rather less against the working-class child when fee-paying places in grammar schools were abolished. However, if the aim of 'secondary education for all' was pursued in practice with a certain lack of vigour, it was nevertheless significant that one major political party had already by 1916 rejected the definition of secondary education devised under the influence of Morant, and was calling for a new definition upon egalitarian lines.

Further pressure for revision came from the reappearance of a familiar problem. The senior classes in elementary schools were becoming choked with pupils, who had finished the ordinary elementary course, and many of whom were willing, even eager, to remain at school beyond the age of compulsion if suitable courses could be offered. But elementary schools had neither the staff nor the facilities for such courses. A report on the conditions in senior classes in Nottingham in 1911 revealed the following situation:

The size of classes is often most excessive, at least during the first part of the educational year ... At Berridge Road there are in the first class of the boys' department 109 boys taught in a room accommodating sixty, and, except when the headmaster is assisting, by a single teacher. In the girls' department there are 96 in the first class.

There were 66 senior departments in the town, and in 38 of them Standards V, VI and VII were all taught together as one class; in only two had Standard VII a teacher of its own. The result was that a pupil

is very likely to find when he is eleven or twelve years old that he has practically reached the end of the course of instruction offered by his school, and must henceforth, to a great extent, mark time until he is permitted to leave . . . in many cases both parents and children are quite conscious of the stagnation to which the latter are liable after a year in the first class and children are thus encouraged to leave school at the earliest possible age. Indeed, in view of the conditions which prevail in a number of schools it is really better that they should do so.

The solution to this problem was obviously to hive off senior pupils into separate schools where they could be provided with courses appropriate to their age. In other words a situation had arisen very similar to that which led to the establishment of higher grade schools in the 1880s, except that the phenomenon was this time more general, and that, whereas only a few of the largest school boards had controlled sufficient schools to make a system of central senior schools a practical possibility, many local education authorities were in this position. Thus the question of the provision of 'post-elementary' schooling began to receive serious consideration. It was in this favourable climate of opinion that the Hadow Committee reported in 1926 in favour of a reorganization of the elementary school system to include a complete break for all children at eleven years, when those not selected for secondary schools would be transferred to senior departments to undertake work recognizably different from that of the traditional elementary school.

There was, therefore, considerable dissatisfaction with the settlement of the question of secondary education which was established by the 1902 Act, but there was also much disagreement about how to replace it. One school of thought favoured an extension of the selective system so that more working-class children could pass to grammar school, those who did not do so receiving post-elementary education in schools reorganized on Hadow lines. This may be referred to as the elitist solution, and it left the 1902 Act undisturbed in all essentials, the sharp distinction between the secondary and elementary systems remaining, although transfer from one to the other was made easier and more frequent. This was the official policy of the inter-war period and it involved a clearly understood difference in the prestige of the two systems. The concept of secondary education was still limited to the kind of literary curriculum associated with grammar schools, and the education provided in senior elementary schools was seen as non-secondary and, in the eyes of the public, certainly less desirable.

A second approach was to extend the definition of secondary education to include all education undertaken above a certain age, eleven years being usually taken as the point of division, but to recognize different types of secondary education depending upon the aptitudes and abilities of the pupils. Administratively this answer was not so very different from the first since it was generally understood that the different kinds of secondary education would take place in different kinds of schools. Both systems were also heavily dependent upon the existence of a system of selection which was accurate and generally seen to be fair. They were therefore liable to be undermined when the accuracy of the selection process was put into question. This was the policy which received much support from official reports immediately before and during the Second World War, and which was finally adopted as the official interpretation of the 1944 Act. The supporters of this policy laid great emphasis upon the importance of 'parity of esteem' between the different kinds of school, this emphasis being perhaps the most obvious point of difference between the first and second solution. Unfortunately it proved to be impossible to legislate parity of esteem into existence and the public obstinately continued to regard grammar schools as superior in status to secondary modern or technical schools. It must be said that they were encouraged in this attitude by the Ministry of Education and the local education authorities, which continued to apply a very obvious order of precedence in staffing and equipping different types of school.

The third approach was that all children should proceed to the same school at the age of transfer, on the model of the United States high school system. This may be called the 'egalitarian' or 'comprehensive' approach, although there were, and are, radical differences between advocates of this policy concerning the degree to which egalitarianism was to be carried within the schools. Some proposed various degrees of streaming or setting, while others, more extreme in their opinions, recommended that there should be no streaming at all. However it was worked out in detail this approach involved a complete rejection of the settlement of 1902 and very substantial administrative changes, including, in the long run at least, much new school building. It was only after 1944 that this policy received serious consideration in England, and for many years support for it was limited, largely because it appeared necessarily to involve the establishment of enormous schools. When the early comprehensive schools were set up in London and elsewhere in the 1950s it was thought necessary to build them for 1,500 to 2,000 pupils. Apart from the manifest impossibility of providing and filling units of this size in sparsely populated rural areas, many administrators and teachers felt reservations about the psychological effects of education in schools of this size. The consideration which led the planners to provide such large schools was a calculation of the proportion of pupils in a non-selective school who would remain for V and VI form work. It was assumed that this proportion would remain fairly low, as in the past, so that schools would have to be large if the senior classes were to be big enough for the economic provision of a respectable range of alternative subjects. An important development since the early 1950s, however, is that this proportion has increased far more quickly than was anticipated, and it is now apparent that comprehensive schools can be much smaller than the early ones and yet produce senior classes of an economic size.

In 1975, assuming that political events do not cause some radical reversal of policy, we are moving from a system based upon the second approach to one based upon the third approach. Some of the problems involved in this development will be considered in greater detail in the next chapter, but it is sufficient here to make three points. First, ever since 1902 there has been a steadily increasing tension between an elitist and an egalitarian interpretation of the concept of secondary education, and it is evident that the side that a person takes in this debate is governed by essentially political considerations. This is a question which extends beyond the boundaries of what is generally considered to be 'education'. Second, the establishment of a system of secondary education along egalitarian lines will raise, in an acute form, questions about the content of the secondary school curriculum. Whatever the virtues of the grammar school course, it was never intended for the education of the whole population, and it cannot be said that the secondary modern school has been particularly successful in finding an alternative course of study. In recent years there has been an increasing approximation between the grammar and modern school curricula, at least so far as the more academic streams of the modern school are concerned, but the work of the Newsom Committee and the Schools' Council, among other agencies, reflect a widespread feeling that this question remains to be answered. Third, a new complicating factor has been introduced into the debate by the establishment of middle schools. If the division of education into three levels rather than two becomes at all general it may well be necessary to seek a further redefinition of the functions of schools of all classes.

To conclude, the state of secondary education in 1975 is similar in one respect to that existing immediately before the 1902 Act. The existing interpretation of the function of the secondary school is challenged from several directions, and various alternative redefinitions are being advocated, but no detailed synthesis has so far been worked out.

Secondary education

in consideration of the function of the secondary school is slightly consequential; in certain social, welfare, alternative, predominant their been administrative before detailed confident has as, in themselves, at out.

CHAPTER 8

RECENT DEVELOPMENTS AND THEIR IMPLICATIONS

In this final chapter I propose to survey the history of popular education in England since the Education Act of 1944. This does not purport to be a chronological account of educational events in the period; indeed, it is likely that many events receive no mention. Instead certain trends in the existing situation are selected, some description of their historical antecedents is given, and an attempt is made to draw out their implications for the future. A venture of this kind presents particular problems. It is notoriously difficult to write contemporary history because the writer stands too close to the events he describes to be able to distinguish their significance, and attempts to extrapolate from current tendencies are liable to be ludicrously mistaken. But it is an important part of the argument of this book that current problems are frequently old problems occurring in a new guise, and that, therefore, previous suggestions for their solution are relevant to teachers and administrators. It is, furthermore, argued that educational problems do not just happen, but occur in a context which has social, political, economic and intellectual factors which are historically determined. For these reasons it is thought to be worthwhile to attempt an historical analysis of some aspects of the contemporary educational scene.

The first topic to be considered is the massive development of secondary education since the Second World War. From every point of view there has been a prodigious expansion in this field. To start with pupils stay at school longer; the minimum school leaving age has been raised first to fifteen years, and now to sixteen years, in each case after much hesitation. But the minimum leaving age has become decreasingly relevant since one of the most marked phenomena of recent years has been the increase in the proportion of pupils who remain at school after that age. Between 1950 and 1966 the total school population rose by 24 per cent. In the same period the number of children aged fifteen years and over increased as is shown in the table below.

Number of children aged 15 years and over in full-time attendance at school

1950	290,354		
1961	504,281		
1966	782,027		
School population:	1950	6,314,784	
	1966	7,850,262	

It will be noticed that this represents an increase between 1950 and 1966 of about 170 per cent, and that the increase in numbers during the 1950s, although massive by previous standards, was dwarfed by the expansion since 1960. The same general expansion, and the sharp acceleration since 1960 is apparent if one looks at the number of pupils aged seventeen and over in secondary schools:

Pupils aged 17 years and over in full-time attendance at school

1951	30,686 being $5\frac{1}{2}$ per cent of the age group
1959	37,500 being 7 per cent of the age group
1964	75,700 being $9 \cdot 8$ per cent of the age group

A closely related phenomenon is the increase in the number of pupils who take school leaving examinations. The figures for GCE 'O' level are as shown below.

Passes at O level in individual subjects

Year	Boys	Girls	Total
1951*	218,248	208,790	427,038
1957	363,192	312,219	675,411
1961	516,290	436,393	952,683
1965	665,284	592,399	1,257,683
1967	651,402	605,078	1,256,480

* The General Certificate of Education replaced the General School Certificate in this year.

These figures show a rise of 194 per cent over the period since the General Certificate of Education was instituted, but it appears that the figures have now reached a plateau; the rise since 1960 has been much slower than in the 1950s, and since 1965 a continued slow increase in entries by girls has been balanced by a marginal reduction in entries by boys. This does not mean, of course, that there is a decline in interest in school leaving examinations. In 1965 the Certificate of Secondary Education was introduced as an alternative or supplement to the GCE, and in summer 1967 696,087 entries were made in individual subjects: 94·5 per cent of entrants gained a grade 5 pass or better, and there were 99,291 grade 1 passes, which are generally accepted as equivalent to GCE O level passes. The combined figures for GCE and CSE suggest that the market for O level is more or less saturated and that the CSE is tapping a group of pupils of rather lower academic ability, a group which would not previously have taken a leaving examination, which is what the CSE set out to do in the first place.

The increase at A level has been even more rapid than at O level.

	Passes at A level in individual subjects		
Year	Boys	Girls	Total
1952	53,652	23,783	77,435
1963	130,581	63,672	194,253
1965	164,739	90,049	254,788

At this level the increase has not yet ceased, although it does show clear signs of slowing down; total passes in 1967 were only 19,000 more than in 1965. A very interesting, if not particularly surprising feature of the A level figures is that the proportion of girls passing the examination has increased significantly. Between 1952 and 1965 the number of passes achieved by boys increased by 206 per cent, while the corresponding increase for girls was 275 per cent.

The evidence suggests, therefore, that the increase in the number of pupils who remain at school beyond the statutory leaving age is accelerating at the same time as the increase in the number of entries for O and A level has either ceased or is visibly slowing. The conclusion appears to be that the idea of delayed leaving has been taken up by the 'secondary modern' type of pupil, a suggestion which is borne out by the large and increasing entry for CSE. This must be a source of encouragement to supporters of comprehensive education since it suggests that the distinction between the 'academic' pupil who will wish to remain at school to take leaving examinations and is suitable for a grammar school type of education, and the non-academic pupil who is best suited in a secondary modern school, is becoming blurred. It is also a generally encouraging sign suggesting that, for whatever reason, there is an increasing interest in secondary education among a wide section of the population.

Perhaps the most immediately obvious reason for this phenomenon is the demand of industry and commerce for trained recruits. It would be too much to say that the necessity for technical training was universally recognized today; the experience of some of the new industrial training boards proves that this is not the case, but it is certainly true that there has never been a time when the attitude of the public towards education has been so favourable as it has been since the Second World War. This is so at the individual level where there is an increasing demand for courses leading to recognized qualifications, at the industrial level where technical qualifications are increasingly required for recruitment and promotion, and at the national level where there is more talk than ever before of education as national investment.

This notion of education as national investment has given a new meaning to the demand for 'relevance' in the curriculum. A standard criticism of school syllabuses is that they have been 'irrelevant' in that they failed to make contact with the interests of children, and merely stocked their minds with useless lumber – 'inert ideas' as A. N. Whitehead put it. Now, however, the idea is floated that schoolwork is only 'relevant' when it prepares pupils for useful work in society upon leaving school. In this way woodwork and metal work, which have generally been given an artistic bias in English schools, are combined with science to produce 'technology', and the Schools Council produces a project for the teaching of 'Humanities', which upon close examination, looks depressingly like the now unfashionable 'citizenship' under a more respectable label.

At the same time the idea has arisen of diverting pupils away from those overstocked subjects like history and modern languages towards scarcity subjects such as the physical sciences. This idea has particular importance in higher education as well as in secondary schools, for the universities have a perennial glut of artists and social scientists and a corresponding shortage of scientists and technologists. Obviously there is nothing in itself absurd or malignant about this scheme; there is no self-evident virtue in an educational system which habitually turns out highly qualified men and women who have no prospect of making use of their qualifications. But discussions upon this topic seem to centre upon the relative return upon the community's investment in training a social scientist or a technologist, and there is serious talk of using the system of student grants to direct students into socially useful studies.

Another subject which has aroused a new interest as the result of the tendency to look at education from a commercial point of view is the cost-efficiency of educational institutions and the economic use of plant. It is noted that school, college and particularly university buildings are only in use for three-quarters or less of the year, and the question is posed whether more economic use could not be made of this very large capital outlay. Some experiments have in fact been carried out in technical colleges and colleges of education, which involve using the buildings for a greater proportion of the year, although these have encountered very strong opposition from staff and students, while many new schools buildings serve two purposes, being used as youth clubs or community centres in the evenings.

Much the largest item in the current expenditure of a school is the salary of the staff and one of the recurrent questions in the history of education is whether the teaching power can be deployed more economically by the use of mechanical or other aids; the monitorial system, of course, was a classical solution to this problem. In recent years suggestions have been made that the use of teaching machines or of unqualified auxiliaries would free the teacher from routine work and allow him to concentrate his efforts where they were most needed. Neither of these suggestions has been enthusiastically received but the likelihood is that both will be adopted far more generally than at present, particularly in view of the fact that the indications are that the Department of Education and Science is looking for evidence to justify abandoning the campaign to reduce the size of classes; colleges of education are already under pressure to reduce their ratio of staff to students. Similarly one of the justifications of the move towards fewer and larger schools is that, particularly at the upper end of the school, it allows for wider alternatives and greater specialization without producing uneconomically small groups.

A rather different effect of the economic analysis of education is the demand that the work of the schools should be measurable – that they should be seen to be giving value for money. This is one of the most important reasons for the contemporary cult of the external examinations, and it is seen in its most lunatic manifestation in the league table of open scholarship results achieved by different schools which is published annually by certain newspapers. The immense increase in the number of pupils and students who take recognized external examinations, which was illustrated above, is indeed one of the most remarkable phenomena of the post-war educational world. The tripartite secondary school system was based explicitly upon the assumption that external examinations would be taken by only a minority of pupils – those at grammar and perhaps technical schools. Secondary modern schools were encouraged to devise courses suitable for pupils who would not take a leaving examination. By the early 1960s this assumption was no longer tenable and the institution of the Certificate of Secondary Education was an official recognition of this fact. But the increase in the demand for school leaving certificates is not an isolated phenomenon. It must be seen in the context of an equally rapid increase in the number of degrees awarded and of a thriving market in technical and commercial qualifications, national certificates and diplomas, and awards of the Royal Society of Arts, the City and Guilds of London Institute and numerous other awarding bodies. Many of these specialist qualifications, national diplomas to take only one example, are inventions of the post-war period. Over an ever-increasing field pupils, students and employers insist upon proof that a specified standard of training and education has been reached, and they demand that the proof will take the form not of a head-teacher's report, but of a certificate of what at least purports to be an independent examining body.

Education is thus increasingly regarded as an industry and assessed by industrial or commercial criteria. This is not a new phenomenon. History books frequently and rightly describe the monitorial system as the factory system worked out in an educational institution, and 'payment by results' was avowedly an application of commercial methods to educational administration. It is an ironical reflection that one of the features of late nineteenth-century secondary schooling against which pioneers of 'progressive' education revolted was the system of external examinations, then in its infancy. It was pointed out in chapter 2 that one of the recurrent reasons for interest in education in England was the needs of industry and commerce, and never has this motive operated more powerfully than at the present time.

But the contemporary expansion of secondary education is not caused only by the need for qualified recruits for industry. There are also political motives at work. The point was made in chapter 7 that from early in the century there has been a demand that secondary education be extended to the whole population and not confined to those pupils who attend grammar school, and one result of the 1944 Act was to make the provision of secondary education for all a legal requirement. Up to a point this change is merely one of name. Long before the 1944 Act pupils within the elementary system were receiving recognizably secondary education either in selective central or senior schools or in the senior departments of ordinary elementary schools, but in the current terminology this was classed as 'higher elementary' schooling, since 'secondary' schooling was, by definition, what was done in a grammar school. The official introduction of secondary education for all has, however, meant a change in fact as well as in name. For one thing the all-age school has disappeared and all pupils pass on to secondary school for part of their education, although the recent introduction of middle schools and sixth-form colleges makes it difficult to say how long they will remain there and at what age their secondary schooling will begin. The huge increase in the number of pupils sitting leaving examinations, and in the number remaining after fifteen years who do not sit examinations makes it obvious that parents and pupils are taking secondary education more seriously than ever before. The Newsom Report made much of the apathy and hostility of children towards school, and for the purposes of its enquiry it was probably right to do so, but from the historical point of view it is necessary to point out that apathy and hostility have been the children's reaction to school from as far back as one cares to investigate. This is not a new development. What is new and interesting is that a vastly greater proportion of children than ever before is indicating that it finds something of value at school, even if this is only the prospect of acquiring a recognized qualification.

Underlying this new acceptance of continued attendance at school is one of the recurrent themes of educational history. This is that the most effective way to create a demand for education is to educate people. In the nineteenth century the advocates of elementary education for the masses frequently argued that to give the working class an elementary education would help to make them contented with their lot. Sceptics, on the other hand took the view that education would have exactly the opposite effect. The possession of an elementary education would lead working men to further study, and even to such dangerous topics as politics and religion. In the event the sceptics were absolutely right. As soon as elementary education became universal, as it did in the 1870s, pressure upon the upper classes of schools led to experiments in quasi-secondary education, and the attempt which followed the 1902 Act to draw a clear distinction between the elementary and secondary fields failed because of the appearance of a post-elementary stage of schooling which received the support of the Hadow Committee and which was manifestly 'secondary' in everything but name. The same internal pressure is the chief reason for the abandonment of the attempt, after 1944, to restrict leaving examinations to grammar schools.

The expansion of secondary education to cover the whole population raises a number of problems. First, what kind of education is suitable for the pupil who leaves at the minimum age and goes straight to work? It is gratifying that the proportion of pupils who elect to remain at school should rise, but the fact remains that the majority do not do so and lack the extrinsic motivation to attend to their school work which is added by an external examination. Until well into the school board period this was no problem; education for the large majority comprised a grounding in the three 'R's and a large measure of socialization. Pupils remained at school for so short a period and frequently came from an environment so hostile to learning that no more could be attempted. Pupils now remain at school for a minimum of ten years, soon to be eleven, and teachers face a very real problem in devising schemes of work for the non-academic child. Various solutions to this problem have been proposed – to make the last year or so in school 'outward-looking', closely related to life outside, with much of the pupil's time spent in extra-mural occupations; to give the school course an explicitly vocational bias. This is not the place to discuss future plans. It is enough to say that the question has yet to be answered how best to give to the non-academic child an education which is recognizably secondary, that is to say that it is not merely an extension of primary school activities in a new building, and which holds the attention of the pupil without collapsing into triviality and entertainment.

The last point is significant because education is a very expensive business. Expenditure of public money upon education in England and Wales comfortably exceeds £2,500 million per year, and it is reasonable that taxpayers should ask whether they are receiving value for this enormous outlay. It has already been suggested that the contemporary enthusiasm for external examinations derives in part from uneasiness on this point. The tendency for pupils to remain longer at school involves yet more expense and the position may be reached where it is asked whether the country can afford to foot the bill. This is a question which naturally applies with particular force to higher education and serious suggestions are now being canvassed that economies may be made by, for example, exercising selection in the award of grants or by converting grants into repayable loans.

It has been assumed in this discussion that external examinations are of proved value as a means of selection and as objectives for school work. In fact this assumption is very dubious. In the first place one may question whether it is desirable that the process of education should be directed towards extrinsic ends such as the passing of an examination. One may further suspect that the enthusiasm for examinations is based upon confusion between the 'educated' man and the 'informed' man. But on a very practical plane there are grounds for doubting the reliability and validity of examinations of the nature of GCE and CSE, to say nothing of degree examinations. Once again this is not the place for detailed discussion of a matter which is the subject of specialist controversy, but it is ironic that after more than thirty years of sustained and well documented assault the 'traditional' examination should be more firmly entrenched than ever, while the 'objective' test appears to have shared in the obloquy poured upon the '11+'.

The expansion of higher education has more than kept pace with developments in the secondary sphere. In 1939 there were eleven universities in England and six university colleges, most of the latter awarding London degrees; there are now thirty-three universities, fourteen of which received their charters in the 1960s. The number of students shows a corresponding rise:

Full-time undergraduate students at university, England and Wales			
Year	Men	Women	Total
1953/4	42,098	13,816	55,914
1960/61	55,134	18,091	73,225
1967/8	98,058	38,109	136,167

It will be observed that the substantial rise of the 1950s was dwarfed by the rise of the 1960s, which is what one might expect from the increase in the number of universities in the period. The new universities of the 1950s were pre-War university colleges which now achieved university status; only Keele, which did not receive its charter until 1962 was a post-War establishment. The 1960s, in contrast, saw the appearance of a large number of new institutions, associated with the major change in government policy regarding higher education which was marked by the Robbins Report.

The developments in the university field formed only a part of the massive post-War expansion in higher education. There has also been a great increase in the amount of advanced work leading to degrees and similar qualifications, which is done outside the universities. The current establishment of polytechnics is one of the most interesting ventures in this direction, since these are institutions where nothing but advanced work is done, much of it to higher degree level and beyond. In other words it is a little difficult to see why they are not given the title of 'university'. On a more modest plane the establishment of the B.Ed. has allowed Colleges of Education to secure a foothold in the degree field. The general tendency, and this again is an innovation of the 1960s is to break down the very sharp distinction between universities where degrees are taken, and other institutions which work for diplomas, associate-ships, certificates, etc.

As one might expect the reasons for this huge expansion of higher education are closely related to those which caused the contemporary expansion in secondary sphere. The autonomous expansion of education is an important factor; as a greater proportion of the population receives an effective secondary education there is an increase in the number of people qualified and competent to enter higher education, and not only are these people qualified to enter universities and colleges, but their levels of aspiration have been raised by secondary education so that they expect to do so. This factor is likely to prove cumulative since parents who receive university education are inclined to expect their children to do likewise.

The high demand for marketable qualifications also has much to do with the pressure upon university accommodation. It is not only a matter of more people working for the traditional kind of qualification. In many trades and professions it is now necessary to hold certificates and diplomas where previously any training that existed was acquired by 'sitting next to Nellie'. In addition there is a progessively increasing demand for qualifications over and above the basic training necessary to pursue a profession, while the standard of the basic training is frequently raised. The teaching profession illustrates this process exactly. The original basic training for teachers was acquired by a two-year course. This was raised to three years in 1963, and from 1968 some teachers emerged from colleges with B.Ed. degrees. In the meantime it was becoming necessary for those teachers who wished for promotion to improve upon their certificates by taking supplementary specialist courses, or by studying for diplomas of advanced study in education, and more recently still there has been a marked rise in the number of teachers who carry their studies yet further to the M.Ed., so that some univer-sities have adjusted their courses to take account of the fact that many of the holders of M.Ed. degrees will remain as teachers or college lecturers rather than continuing in research. These developments within teaching only mirror changes on a wider front. Until well after the Second World War the first degree was the ultimate goal of the vast majority of university students; only those continued who were taking specialized post-graduate certificates, teachers for example, or who proposed to follow a career of research or scholarship. One of the features of modern university life is that the post-graduate population is growing significantly faster than the undergraduate population.

Full time post-graduate students at university, England and Wales

Year	Men	Women	Total
1953/4	8,441	2,249	10,690
1960/1	12,713	3,232	15,945
1967/8	24,960	6,625	31,585

Undoubtedly this is related to the fact that possession of a first degree does not carry the weight that it did even a few years ago. There are far more first degrees about, and competition requires the taking of higher qualifications. This argument can be driven too far however. Another interesting feature of university life – this point has been touched upon before – is that the most intense pressure for places is not in those departments, the sciences and technologies for example, where degrees have the greatest market value, but in the arts and social sciences where the prospects of relevant employment are poor. Apparently there are other factors than the quest for saleable certificates at work here.

Another factor of prime importance in the developments of the 1960s has been the official acceptance of a new approach to higher education. Essentially the traditional English attitude has been that university education is for a small, intensively selected intellectual elite, and that the bulk of higher education would take place outside universities, in technical colleges, colleges of education and so on which would adopt a strongly vocational bias, university education being liberal in nature. The distinction between the two branches of higher education was marked by the award, by universities only, of a degree. This distinction was always a difficult one to defend. For one thing it proved to be impossible to make much sense of the difference between liberal and vocational courses. For another, the 'red-brick' universities, Manchester, Birmingham, Nottingham, etc., had all started their careers as technical colleges, and although they had risen in the world they retained some embarrassing reminders of their origin, agricultural colleges for example, and courses in such blatantly vocational subjects as pharmacy, textiles, brewing and education. Nevertheless in the late 1950s an attempt was made to devise a stratified system of higher education with a limited number of universities, supported by Colleges of Advanced Technology, which awarded not a degree but a diploma in technology which was supposed to carry the same status. The 1960s saw the adoption of a totally different policy based upon what may be described as the American approach to higher education. This is based upon two premises, first that higher education will be provided for all comers; second that all institutions of higher education will be classed as universities. Characteristically the English accepted these premises in a half-hearted manner, nearly doubling the number of universities, partly by promoting colleges of advanced technology, but retaining a stratified system of higher education with polytechnics, colleges of education, colleges of technology and many other institutions occupying various positions in the hierarchy. One of the questions which will have to be faced in the next few years is whether the distinction between universities and polytechnics can be made to hold, or whether, like the similar distinction between universities and CATs it will prove to be a distinction without a difference.

Acceptance of the American system of higher education, even if in a very modified manner, is clearly a victory for egalitarianism over elitism. Not only are new institutions given the status of university, but courses and subjects now enjoy the cachet of degree status which previously could only be studied for certificates or diplomas. Education is a case in point, and one of the difficulties in the way of floating the B.Ed. was that nobody, in university or elsewhere, knew what a first degree in education should look like. A certificate they understood, or a second degree, but a first degree was an entirely new venture. This fact accounts in large measure for the variety of practice at the different universities in preparing for and awarding the degree. It is a further indication of the change in attitude which has occurred towards higher education that while the older university colleges like Exeter, Leicester and Keele had to serve a long apprenticeship before being granted their charters, the new wave of universities of the 1960s received theirs immediately.

Changes of this magnitude inevitably cause problems, particularly where they are not wholeheartedly welcomed so that there is a division among those in authority over major matters of policy. One fundamental question, which has already been referred to in connection with secondary education, is whether the country can continue to afford to provide higher education for all comers under the present system of grants. It may be that it will be necessary, if the number of students continues to rise at the present rate, to abandon the system by which the award of a grant is effectively automatic upon offer of a place at university or college. This is a point at which the two philosophies of higher education clash, and where the English refusal to make a definite commitment to one side or the other causes serious confusion. The elitist philosophy envisaged higher education as provided for a relatively small proportion of the population, which made it a reasonable economic proposition that the minority which passed the selection process should receive substantial grants. The egalitarian philosophy, by contrast, sees higher education as the natural continuation to secondary schooling and available to all-comers. In England, in point of fact, there appears to be some doubt whether higher education should be provided as a right for everyone, or only for everyone who qualifies, but however the rubric is interpreted it involves a dramatic increase in the number of students, and this must raise the question whether a new policy is required over student grants.

A second question concerns the type of course offered by universities and colleges. For various reasons there has been much discussion since the War on the nature of first degree courses, but the problem has now extended to higher degrees. The English higher degree has in the past been based upon research and the presentation of a thesis, which is a sensible enough arrangement on the assumption that the vast majority of candidates for such degrees are intending to continue in a career of scholarship. This assumption is no longer valid and the universities are experimenting with higher degrees by examination for students who require the degrees for the sake of further promotion.

A group of problems is related to the tendency of students to stay longer at college. A teacher in training, for example, who was following a two-year course at a training college could, if he found the college administration frustrating, endure for this relatively short period for the purpose of obtaining a certificate. This is more difficult to do as the course is extended to three years, and for B.Ed. students to four years, and it is not unreasonable that students should demand some say in the management of institutions where they may stay for longer than a good proportion of the staff. The students' demands for a measure of control are reinforced by the political climate which favours 'participation' in the process of government.

A particular problem relates to post-graduate students who form an increasing proportion of the student population. One may question whether there is not a tendency for studentship to become a semi-permanent status rather than a preparation and whether, in some cases, registration for a further course is not a way of avoiding the responsibilities and competition of life outside the educational system. Certainly one of the significant social developments of recent years has been the delaying of the completion of full-time education for the whole population, and particularly for those, an increasing proportion, who seek particular qualifications. Raising the school leaving age and vastly increasing the student population both tend in this direction, and it will be necessary in the future to give some thought to the economic, political and legal status of the student, particularly in view of the increasing independence of young people and the political power which has recently been given to the eighteen to twenty-one age group, which may be thought to render obsolete the protective atmosphere of many educational institutions.

Throughout this book attention has been drawn to the way in which, partly by design and partly through force of circumstances, control of education has been centralized. By and large, in the nineteenth century this was an accidental process. The government was drawn first into elementary and later into secondary and higher education without any conscious policy, and often very much against its wishes. Thus payment by results was initiated as an attempt to decentralize the control of elementary education and the disastrous vacillation of the Education Department with regard to higher grade schools in the 1880s and 1890s was due not only to ineptitude but also to a conscientious reluctance to dictate policy to the school boards. From the time of Morant onwards the Board of Education pursued a more active policy – the change of title being symptomatic of a new attitude, as were the later changes to Ministry of Education and Department of Education and Science. Since 1944 innovation in education has increasingly tended to be initiated from the centre. For example, the tripartite system of secondary education was established as the result of the interpretation placed upon the 1944 Act by the Ministry of Education, while the more recent move towards comprehension is notoriously being pressed by the government upon reluctant local education authorities. Similarly, in higher education the establishment of colleges of advanced technology and their subsequent abandonment in favour of enlarging the university system were carried through as part of the policy of the government of the day, in marked contrast to the spontaneous appearance of the municipal universities – Birmingham, Leeds, etc. – in the 1870s. In teacher training the three-year basic training and the B.Ed. were both instituted by the Department of Education and Science, and it is well known that the enthusiasm of the department for the degree was greater than that of some of the universities, which required some pressure before they would set up the machinery for awarding it. The recommendations of the Weaver Report upon government of colleges of education were also clearly more palatable to the Department than to local education authorities which lost a measure of their control over the colleges. Finally both Conservative and Labour ministers have insisted upon interfering vigorously in the decisions of the Burnham Committee, thus making nonsense of any claim it might make to be an independent negotiating body.

Of course it is not meant to imply that all educational ideas actually originate with the government any more now than they have ever done. The change which has occurred is that the department is now willing, even eager to disseminate ideas which are brought to its notice, to establish machinery to make easier such dissemination, and, on occasion, to bring some pressure to bear for the acceptance of these ideas. Sometimes, as with the introduction of comprehension, educational changes are initiated directly as a part of a larger programme of social reform, and here also there has been a greater willingness since the War to accept the government's right to adopt an active role.

One reason for the increased power of the government is the ever-rising cost of education. It was already evident as early as the 1890s that the board schools, which received rate aid, were drawing ahead of the voluntary schools, which did not, in buildings, equipment and staffing, and one of the motives for the passing of the 1902 Act was to find a way of giving rate aid to voluntary schools. Now the position has been reached that not even local education authorities can afford to pay the cost of the educational services without massive support from the central government, which finds itself more or less obliged to call the tune whether it wishes to do so or not. But another reason is that the long swing from individualism to collectivism has almost been completed so that the nineteenth-century objection to government inititative in social legislation, and fear of increasing the power of the government in the affairs of the individual citizen have been abandoned. Clearly this is not a change which is peculiar to education. On the contrary this is just one proof of the fact that the history of education is a branch of social history and cannot properly be understood out of context. The increasing control of the government in education is related particularly to the acceptance in Britain of the concept of the welfare state, where education, along with medical attention, pensions, etc., is no longer a matter of personal investment but has become the responsibility of the community at large.

The full implications of this change have not yet been worked out in England; it is doubtful whether it is fully appreciated by the public how far the change towards collectivism has gone. Furthermore the implications of accepting collectivism are not clear. To take a concrete case; if the state has the duty to provide secondary and higher education for its members, does it also have the right to call upon their services when their education is completed? Is the money spent upon their education to be viewed as a gift to which they are unconditionally entitled, or as an investment upon which the state may expect a return? In communist states where the theory of collectivism has been most completely worked out, it has been assumed that an educated person owes his services to the state, and may be directed to work, at least within limits at the state's convenience. But although this answer is perfectly sensible, it is not logically necessary, and, as was pointed out in the discussion of higher education, the English answer remains to be found. Similarly, must education in a collective state be egalitarian? In recent years we have moved away from the concept of education as a process of progressive selection with the majority of pupils weeded out early on, towards a concept of education as self-selection with pupils remaining as long as they wish, the only restriction being upon the minimum period one remains at school. This kind of concept lies behind such administrative schemes as the Leicestershire plan and behind the contemporary demands of students that higher education be a right rather than a privilege with little, if any, assessment of students' performance. On the other hand it is interesting to note that the Russian educational system is intensely competitive with a more rigorous selection process than has ever existed in England. Once again no answer has yet been formulated to this question, but, unfortunately, it is more than likely that both the questions posed in this paragraph will soon be answered on economic, rather than specifically educational, grounds.

So far we have been concerned with the effects of increased state control upon educational administration. But one of the most conspicuous developments of the last ten years has been the increased interference with the way a teacher teaches. The independence of the teacher has probably always been more potential than actual unless he was a head-teacher or taught in one of those grammar schools where the head thought it unprofessional to supervise his staff closely. Most teachers have usually been subject to a considerable degree of dictation from heads, and possibly from heads of department; if they were working towards an examination they had the syllabus laid down for them, and text-books have often been a limiting factor. Still it was possible for a resolute teacher who was no respecter of persons to achieve a measure of independence which would astonish teachers in France, for example, and every teacher enjoyed considerable scope in the way he taught individual lessons. The syllabus or text-book might dictate the content, but the method could usually be varied within wide limits.

This freedom has been eroded from two directions. On the one side there is a strong tendency for new media of instruction to limit the area for innovation on the teacher's part. This is not always intentional, but in the case, for example, of a series of television programmes it is necessary for the teacher to keep fairly close to the master plan if the class is to make much sense of succeeding instalments, and this may have an accidentally cramping effect. With programmed learning the effect is more deliberate. The point of programming is that the method of learning as well as the content is laid down by the programmer, thus allowing an increased degree of self-instruction, and removing the necessity for constant attention by the teacher. The advantage of this in allowing a teacher to concentrate his efforts where they are most needed is obvious, but the fact must not be overlooked that the whole direction of the work lies in the hands of the writer of the programme, and, in practice, this will very often not be the teacher. Of course it is possible to argue that an important point in favour of programming is that it can be conducted successfully even in the absence of a teacher who is fully conversant with the subject. Where, as is often the case, there is a shortage of teachers of real authority this is a powerful argument, but it serves to underline the original point of this section which is that the planning of a course of lessons is being removed from the hands of teachers, who are tending to become agents of other people's plans. This tendency has not yet gone very far, but it exists and is not often recognized.

The increasing structuring of the media of teaching is casual and unco-ordinated. One would have to be paranoid to suspect a plot upon the independence of the teacher. Far more organized, and at the present time far more successful, is the campaign to induce teachers to surrender their independence voluntarily. This is a very recent development, and has made great progress working chiefly through the Schools Council and the teachers' centres which are being founded all over the country. The approach is to bring teachers together locally, regionally or nationally to discuss problems and suggest solutions, which, in the case of the Schools Council are often published in bulletins and working papers. It is important to preserve a sense of proportion in discussing this development. Individualism is not necessarily a virtue if it leads to inefficiency. One of the problems facing a teacher is the difficulty of finding out how other teachers tackle their job, and a teachers' centre or the publications of Schools Council provide valuable opportunities to widen his experience; few teachers would claim that they have nothing to gain from a professional discussion with their colleagues. But it is notorious that discussion groups can be converted with alarming ease into devices for exerting peer-group pressure upon non-conformists. This is a fact well known to Wesley when he established the class system in the Methodist movement, and the Communist party has always used this system to maintain party discipline. Perhaps it seems fanciful to speak of the Schools Council, for example, as a device for bringing pressure to bear upon teachers and yet this is precisely how the Schools Council sees itself.

The terms of reference laid down when the Schools Council was founded are as follows:

The objects of the School Council for the Curriculum and Examinations are to uphold and interpret the principle that each school should have the fullest possible measure of responsibility for its own work, with its own curriculum and teaching methods based on the needs of its own pupils and evolved by its own staff; and to seek through cooperative study of common problems, to assist all who have individual or joint responsibility for, or in connection with, the schools' curricula or examinations to co-ordinate their actions in harmony with this principle.

These terms of reference are quoted in *The First Three Years*, an account published by the council of its activities between 1964 and 1967. In the same pamphlet the council interprets its duties in the following words: 'The job entrusted to the Schools Council in 1964 was, basically to find ways and organize means of reviewing – and reforming – the school curriculum in England and Wales.' Now what has happened to the principle which received such emphasis in 1964 – 'that each school should have the fullest possible measure of responsibility for its own work, with its own curriculum and teaching methods . . . ?' The interesting point is that the authors of *The First Three Years* do not seem to appreciate that there is a radical incompatibility between their statement of 'the job entrusted to the Schools Council', and the terms of reference which they themselves quote. Once again this is not a sinister conspiracy to subvert the teacher. The point is that an important change is occurring in English education, and it appears to be occurring, as so often is the case, by accident rather than as the result of policy. Payment by results imposed a massive uniformity of content and method upon popular education. A reaction set in almost immediately, and after 1902 the Board of Education gave powerful support to the movement for diversification of teaching method. In the words of the *Handbook of Suggestions for Teachers*, which have been previously quoted: 'The only uniformity of practice that the Board of Education desires to see in the teaching of Public Elementary Schools is that each teacher shall think for himself, and work out for himself such methods of teaching as may use his powers to the best advantage and be best suited to the particular needs and conditions of the school.'

This is the philosophy which has governed official and unofficial views on teaching methods until very recently. It still receives lip service from educationalists, administrators and teachers; the terms of reference of the School Council echo the *Handbook of Suggestions* in their emphasis on the autonomy of the individual school and teacher. But, in hard fact, the movement is towards a substantial degree of 'uniformity of practice' although the pressures upon the teacher are now less crude than in the days of payment by results. This is very natural in the age of the planned society, but it is none the less a major change in the concept of the role of the teacher.

In chapter 8 I attempted, from the viewpoint of 1970, some analysis of the contemporary educational scene, with the intention of distinguishing what appeared to be the more important trends, and, possibly, of predicting their future developments. Change in education has been so rapid in the 1970s that it is now appropriate to revise this analysis, noting where predictions have been verified, explaining, so far as possible, where they have been conspicuously inaccurate, and seeking for significant new tendencies. Such an analysis must be offered – and received – with caution, for the events of the past five years emphasize how extremely difficult it is to predict educational developments, or indeed to make sense of what is happening now.

One constant factor at least can be detected. Public interest in education remains, by historical standards, abnormally high, and may even be higher in 1975 than in 1970. The many-sided power struggle, which must receive separate attention, has kept the issue of control of educational policy at all levels before the public, the special case of comprehensivization versus selection arousing particularly powerful feelings. Fierce public controversy, with similar political overtones has been stirred by the debate concerning the future of direct grant and independent schools. In both cases the classes of people especially affected are those most articulate and most accomplished in the organization of opinion. They may be relied upon to make sure that their grievances receive the maximum advertisement in the press and other media.

A different source of publicity for educational issues is the discussion over increased violence in schools. How far there really has been such an increase is hard to determine. Violence and intimidation are certainly not new to schools. They were endemic in elementary schools of the nineteenth and early twentieth centuries, as G.A.N. Lowndes makes clear in *The Silent Social Revolution*, to take only one instance. Urban secondary modern schools of the 1940s and 1950s also took the presence of a violent minority of pupils as one of the facts of pedagogical life, unpleasant but inevitable. Nor have public and grammar schools always been centres of peaceful, orderly searching after learning, a fact well known to writers of school stories and memoirs of school life, whether ex-pupils or ex-teachers. To an extent, at least, excitement over pupil violence is factitious, stirred up deliberately, either by teachers' unions hoping to draw attention to their members' difficulties, or by defenders of selection looking for a stick with which to beat the comprehensives.

Nevertheless certain recent changes have operated to bring pupil violence into the open, even if they have not increased its incidence. In the past active hostility to schooling and actively anti-social behaviour have been largely confined to urban secondary modern schools, particularly those in what would now be called 'educational priority areas', where their effects were concealed from any but the most penetrating eye, and where, as I have suggested, the teachers accepted them as a normal aspect of school routine. Now, comprehensivization has brought the disaffected element into schools patronized by the children of politicians, business and professional men, councillors, journalists, many of whom are already dubious about the social and academic consequences of abandoning selection. Levels of expectation, too, have risen, although this is a much longer-standing process. Bullying, fighting, and overt hostility to education, which the Victorians took for granted, are no longer tolerated, probably because we no longer draw the sharp distinction which they drew between children's conduct on duty and off. Discipline in Victorian schools could be draconian, but teachers limited their jurisdiction to pupils' behaviour in the classroom. What children did in their spare time was their own business, and it was assumed that their extra-curricular activities would often be mischievous at the very least. One of the most significant educational developments of post-War years has been the increasing scope claimed by formal schooling, a trend clearly reflected in the wider definitions given in educational literature to the term 'curriculum'. As schools have widened their claims to control the emotional, social, recreational and even political development of children, so, very naturally, have public expectations of their achievement risen accordingly.

But, whether or not schools really are more violent places than they were, discussion of violence certainly has important consequences. It helps to create the very phenomenon that is feared by introducing hitherto docile pupils to the possibilities of violence, while encouraging the disaffected with the promise of publicity. At the same time it serves to keep education before the public eye, if only as a source of potential trouble. It may even – as the National Association of Schoolmasters clearly understands – enhance the prospects of teachers by endowing them with 'front line' status. On the other hand it provides ammunition both for those who call for a more precise accountability for schools, and for the more radical critics who question the practicability of using schools to produce massive social reforms. Evidence of what at least appears to be failure by schools may be used for two quite contradictory purposes – as an argument for more intensive schooling with more explicit social and political training, or as a reinforcement for the view that schools cannot or should not attempt such training at all.

Tension between central and local government over control of educational policy is another continuing factor: indeed the dispute over comprehensivization and selection has reached the point of direct confrontation in certain areas which stubbornly refuse to implement plans for the abolition of selection. This dispute raises with peculiar clarity the fundamental issue in this field: how far can, or should, central government insist upon imposing national policies against the opposition of local authorities, a very sensitive question at a time when reservations are being voiced in many quarters about the preponderant power of the government and its neglect of local interests.

Two factors complicate this issue. The cost of education continues to rise, constituting much the largest item of expenditure in either central or local government, and the suggestion is made with increasing frequency that it should cease to be a charge on the local rates at all, the whole burden being borne by taxation. Since a large and increasing proportion of the cost is already met from central funds, this suggestion has a certain logical weight. But it has worrying implications that have so far prevented its adoption. To make education chargeable solely to national funds would, it is argued, be to assert that it is a national, not a local concern, and this would be contrary to a tradition of division of power which arguably extends back to the first appearance of state intervention in education in the 1830s. Local authorities would become simply agents for the administration of centrally determined policies, financed by central resources.

Local government reorganization is a second complication, but it is too early yet to say precisely what its effects will be. On the one hand it might be supposed that larger local authorities might be more belligerent and independent; certainly this has been the case in the past. But on the other, is the fact that reorganization has reduced the size of some of the traditionally independent authorities – Lancashire for example – and has created others which possess, as yet, no sense of identity, or which even combine communities distinguished by traditional mutual hostility. It is possible, too, that the political compromises necessary to reconcile the claims of old authorities as they were subsumed under new groupings, may produce weaknesses of leadership both on the elected and the professional sides.

Power struggles in education are not confined to relations between central and local government. The autonomy of individual teachers continues to be eroded, by massively enlarged local advisory staffs, through demands for accountability to local authorities, through the popularity of corporate planning and the spread of teachers' centres. Teachers themselves are frequently the most enthusiastic advocates of the devices which reduce their own power and status. They argue that, in the planning of new courses and examinations, teachers through panels and committees are consulted more fully than ever before and that their expertise has received a new level of recognition. In a sense this is true. There is today a more comprehensive system of discussion and consultation, involving teachers along with administrators and academics. But the critical point missed by such arguments is that while teachers, as a body, are formally represented on planning committees, the actual power of individual teachers is eroded, since they are required to conform to the committees' decisions in detail. This, rather than the consultation, is what is really new, since until very recently it was assumed that each school, and even each teacher would solve his problems in his own way, an attitude which allowed scope for inefficiency to be sure, but also allowed the genuine individualist to work out his ideas without the need to convince a committee. It may be that such organizations as the Schools' Council will succeed in institutionalizing inventiveness, but it seems far more likely that they will serve the purpose of domesticating the inconveniently original and nonconformist. At a time when 'radicalism' means not fundamental criticism but the unquestioning acceptance of pre-packed political doctrine this will seem to many a desirable result.

The belief that representation of teachers upon committees and panels means increased strength represents a double confusion. It is possible for the profession as a whole to gain strength while individual teachers lose their autonomy. In this case the general gain is very dubious, but the individual loss is perfectly obvious. But the more important confusion is between formal and actual power. In the 1960s teachers, along with students, parents and pupils were concerned to gain a place in the formal power structure. They sought for representation upon academic boards and governing bodies, for official channels of consultation in planning, for the establishment of school moots and councils with judicial and legislative power, and considerable progress was made in this direction, especially in higher education. But experience has shown that 'worker participation' is not the expected panacea, that there remains a very awkward gap between 'representative' and 'participatory' democracy. Indeed, universities and colleges have discovered, like industry in earlier days, that acceptance of student representation may be an excellent device for emasculating protest, since the student leaders find themselves in a very weak position when opposing measures for which, as members of academic board or senate, they are responsible. In national politics, disillusionment with representative government, a feeling that individuals and even minorities are helpless against the mass vote and those with the power to influence it, has produced the current enthusiasm for community politics, conceived as direct, participatory democracy in practice. Protest movements gain much of their momentum from the same source, and it is from here in particular that they derive their learning towards violent methods, a natural recourse for a minority which finds that redress through constitutional channels is blocked by immovable majorities. Similar disenchantment is observable in higher education, where student interest in representative devices is low, academic boards, senates and governing bodies being dismissed, not altogether unjustly, on the grounds that student members are in a permanent minority and have little real power.

However, disappointing though representative institutions may often be to those who hoped that they were the key to academic democracy, it is an over-simplification to regard them as simply a confidence trick by the 'establishment', designed to purchase the support of the student body in return for insignificant and largely illusory concessions. One has only to look at colleges of education to see how the changes of the past ten years or so have diminished the direct power of the principal, who now finds himself hedged about by academic boards, students' unions and disciplinary codes. Head-teachers, when discussing students' performance on teaching practice, frequently express surprise at how little control colleges now have over students' activities. Their observations on this topic are normally disapproving, but even heads are just beginning to lose some of their hitherto almost unquestioned internal dominance, although the movement towards greater power for pupils, or even for assistant teachers, makes slow progress compared with similar developments in higher education.

More fundamental is the change in attitudes represented by the attempt to allow pupils and students some voice in the planning and control of their education. It signifies a clear break with the very old and widespread assumption that education is something done to the young, in their own interests perhaps, but probably unpleasant, nonetheless. Traditionally, teachers and parents have taken it for granted that pupils would resent schooling, or at best be indifferent to it, and many went so far as to suppose that schooling not only *was* painful, but *ought* to be so, rather as exercise is effective if it hurts. Although distinguished educators have argued against this belief for centuries, it is only very recently that anything like common acceptance has been accorded to the idea that a teacher is failing if his pupils are hostile or uninterested. Even more recent is the suggestion that pupils should be involved in academic planning.

But, if education is to proceed in an atmosphere of concensus rather than confrontation, some notice must be taken of the interests and preferences of the clients, whether or not they are formally consulted, and this means that the educators may have to accept a considerable dilution of what they think ought to be taught. Many teachers, of course, take the interests of their pupils as a starting point, hoping to catch their attention in order to lead them on towards what they conceive to be more useful or demanding activities. In practice, however, it may often be necessary to compromise between what teachers want to teach and what pupils wish to learn. The more sensitive teachers are about pupils' rights and interests, and the more pupils are encouraged to exert their strength, the more the teachers' message is likely to be diluted.

Public schools discovered this a hundred years ago. Worried by the hostility of pupils to the official school programme, and by the dubious moral tone of the almost independent schoolboy culture, teachers wished to increase the scope and intensity of their influence over the boys. They did so largely by exploiting group loyalty through the house system and by adapting the prefect system to provide support for the school's ethos and discipline. Their success was considerable, demonstrated by their production of an identifiable 'public school' type. But it has been noticed by critics at the time and by historians since, that this was done, not by imposing a set of values upon the boys but by accepting and reinforcing their existing values. The price of pupil support was abandonment of the scholarly ideals of the early nineteenth century public school for worship of athletic prowess, contempt for intellectual values, uncritical group loyalty and intolerance of nonconformity and individualism. Rather similar criticisms are levelled at experiments in 'progressive' secondary education. The pupils, it is alleged, accept school precisely because it is undemanding and their prejudices are not disturbed by demands for fundamental critical thinking. The values of the youth culture are reinforced, but it is a lowest common denominator culture offering no intellectual challenge to the pupils, while insufficient attention is paid to the fact that education has, inevitably, a preparatory function, assisting children to prepare for adult life.

But the thrust of pupil power, formal or informal, is opposed by a drive to increase the influence of schooling seen as an instrument of social engineering. In our intensely and increasingly totalitarian society we are no longer prepared to tolerate dissent or eccentricity and we think it essential that the young be efficiently infected with the values and attitudes proper to whatever new order we advocate. In this the political left and right are in complete agreement. Pupils must not be allowed to misinterpret the message we wish them to acquire, nor to avoid it by absence, or by attendance only in body, as, until very recently, it was assumed that many would do. To achieve this level of educational saturation, however, we must broaden the base of schools' operations; the formal programme of lessons – the curriculum in common parlance – does not provide sufficient leverage, for too much of a pupil's environment is beyond the schools' control. The curriculum must cover a wider segment of pupils' experience, extending far into what has hitherto been considered his private life, while teaching must be more precisely directed and organized to avoid diffusion of the message, or, worse still, varying interpretations by individual teachers.

The schools' attack, therefore, is two-pronged. Increasingly they aim to take over functions traditionally performed – or very often neglected – by parents, the church, or community agencies. Youth clubs and other recreational activities are brought within the schools' orbit, 'pastoral care' becomes a major preoccupation of teachers, acquiring a professional status as 'counselling', and extending far beyond merely academic or career advice. Efforts are made to develop co-operation with the pupils' homes, with social services and with community groups in an attempt to harness the pressure of parents and other adults, whose influence, whether deliberately or not, so often serves to undermine the schools' campaign. Co-ordination between primary and secondary schools, too, is tightened up, and schools become centres for adult classes, clubs and societies, so that the developed community school, theoretically at least, exerts its pressure from cradle to grave.

The academic programme, too, is sharpened to make it a more effective agent of indoctrination. Traditional practices, with teachers operating in separate rooms, and, at the secondary stage, with specialist subjects, are not suitable here. They call for little consultation and only a minimum of co-ordination between teachers, thus allowing a multiplicity of individual interpretations, while detailed central direction is almost impossible. Specialist teachers, too, are often interested only in a relatively limited sector of their pupils' personalities; if they are competent physicists or historians their moral or religious condition, or political persuasion is ignored as being beyond the teacher's sphere of operations. As we have seen, Victorian teachers, until the reforms of the 1870s onwards, were committed to this viewpoint, and often made it a matter of conscience not to enquire into their pupils extra-curricular pursuits.

Modern teaching techniques – integrated studies, team teaching, open-plan schools – are planned specifically to break down both the divisions between subjects and the isolation of individual teachers. Their effect is greatly to increase the schools' impact upon pupils by co-ordinating teachers' efforts and eliminating, or at least minimizing, the possibility of competing messages from different subjects or individual teachers. A side-effect, not always intentional, or even appreciated, is an accession of power to heads and heads of departments, who gain partly from the necessity for formal planning of courses, a rather point-less exercise when individual teachers taught specialist subjects to single classes, and partly from the increased visibility of teaching under the new systems. This again provides an opportunity for schools to increase their efficiency since it provides a check upon dissent or simple incompet-ence on the part of teachers, often very hard to detect under traditional conditions.

These developments are not altogether new; the tendency of schools to widen the scope of their activities may be traced back for a century. Nor is their motivating force always the wish of teachers to increase their power at the expense of parents and others, for the increasing size of schools often necessitates more precise organization of courses and pastoral care. Nevertheless the claims of schools have become so extensive in the 1970s, and the political motives behind community schooling and comprehensive education so explicit – and often so intolerant – that signs of reaction have appeared in several quarters. Some critics argue that schools are attempting to do the impossible, or, to put it another way, that we deceive ourselves if we believe that schools can bring about major social changes unless education is only a part of a much more compre-hensive programme of reform. Others maintain that whether or not schools have such power, it is wrong for them to use it. They argue, for example, that too many educational programmes are based upon the con-cept of 'social deprivation', that is to say that many children – typically from the urban working class – are handicapped because they do not possess the 'richer' culture of the middle classes, and that it is the func-tion of schools to introduce them to this culture, acting as substitutes for their families. Social deprivation, they aver, is a myth. The working-class culture, while different from that of the middle class, is not there-fore necessarily inferior, and schools would do better to concentrate upon developing the culture that children have rather than attempting to 'raise' them to the middle classes, thus very probably cutting them off from their cultural roots. Such a programme is clearly closely related to the demand for 'Black studies' in American higher education and has very similar political implications. It is not a protest against the over-mighty power of schools, but a demand that this power be given a different political complexion.

More radical is the 'de-schoolers' criticism, for they demand, in effect, that schooling be dis-established. Schools, they say – and by this term they mean all institutions of formal education – have extended their functions far beyond their original and legitimate one of passing on skills and information. In consequence they have gained far too much power as instruments of indoctrination, of social and vocational selection, and of custodial care, and have become largely devices for preserving the social and political establishment, while, because of their diffusion of effort, they have become very inefficient at their basic task of instruction. Furthermore the public has been 'educated' into the belief that learning only happens between certain ages and in certain institutions set aside for the purpose. What we must do, it is suggested, is to break with the notion that a person's education finishes when he or she leaves school at sixteen or eighteen and give up the attempt to cram a lifetime's education into eleven years. Compulsory schooling, if it survives, must be limited to the absolute minimum and people be allowed to acquire their learning in or out of school, wherever they feel the need to do so and in whatever topic seems appropriate to them. The use of schooling as an instrument of a social or political programme would be outlawed and the functions of schools would shrink to providing courses upon demand, a situation very similar to that of nineteenth-century private schools. There is, in fact, a very nineteenth-century flavour about the de-schooling proposals which are based upon a highly individualistic view of society, but this is perhaps one of its strengths, since the refusal of the de-schoolers to accept assumptions that we too easily take for granted gives an edge to their criticisms of our practices.

The struggle for power in education is clearly a complex phenomenon. At what we might describe as the 'constitutional' level is the conflict between central and local government. This is complicated by the dispute, to which we have just referred, over how much real power over individual schools is to be allowed to whatever constitutional authority emerges triumphant. In this dispute the forces internal to the school may be grouped together and contrasted with external forces – teachers, parents, and pupils on the one side; local education authority and D.E.S. on the other. This is the approach of community schoolers, for example. But it is perfectly obvious that a school can only be classed as a community if we are prepared to allow that a community can contain a very high concentration of hostility, or, at the very least, of clash of interest, between sub-groups. Whether or not it is true, as many teachers and many sociologists would maintain, that the very nature of the activity of teaching involves inevitable conflict, it is an observable fact that very much teaching proceeds in conditions of armed truce, and that there are many schools and many more individual classes where the truce has worn very thin indeed. Much of the talk of a 'generation gap' that was common a few years ago, was based upon the premise that there existed an unbridgeable gap between what children and young people *were* interested in, and what teachers and others thought they *ought to be* interested in. More recently a political dimension has been added to the discussion by sociologists who have argued that a particular source of tension and hostility lies in the collision between the predominantly middle class values of teachers and the predominantly working class values of the majority of pupils.

But the generation gap does not run simply between teachers and pupils. Parents are divided from their children just as much as teachers. A particular difficulty facing teachers in their search for professional status is that, by comparison with doctors, say, or solicitors, they are not at all certain who are their clients. Leaving aside for the moment the claim of national and local authorities, both parents and children have prima facie cases for assuming this role. And this may put schools in a delicate position, for the interests of parents and children may not run parallel. In fact the institution of compulsory education occurred precisely because the state became aware of a clash between the interests of parents and children that could only be resolved by the intervention of a third party sufficiently powerful to enforce its solution. Here we encounter a problem that has never been squarely faced by de-schoolers and others who argue that power should be transferred from the local authority or the teachers to the consumer. Who is the consumer? Pupils may certainly claim to be so, and parents too. So, in a less direct way may local ratepayers, who pay for schools and employ most of their products. An increase in, for instance, parent control, does not simply mean that parents have greater control over the actions of teachers. It may also mean a significant diminution in the control of the L.E.A., and almost certainly a considerable reduction in the autonomy of pupils.

So far we have spoken of pupils as if they form a homogenous group, but this is manifestly a gross over-simplification. Sixth formers are no more the natural representatives of the interests of eleven year olds than are parents or teachers, or, for that matter, local education authorities. Indeed in the nineteenth century secondary schools where pupil power in the strongest sense was the normal state of affairs, its most obvious manifestation was brutal bullying and intimidation of younger pupils by their older colleagues. Nothing we have heard about conditions in the secondary schools of today suggests that community of interests between groups is more general than it was a hundred years ago.

The same is true of parents. If sociologists are correct in maintaining that social class continues to function as a major divisive agent we can hardly look for unanimity here. The most recent case where parent power has made its voice heard has been in support of selective secondary schooling, and whatever else supporters of selection are asking for, they are certainly demanding distinctive schooling for different classes of pupils, as are parents who support independent schools, and these form the other most vocal parental pressure group. Any head-teacher who has wrestled with a parent–teacher association will have learned at least two important facts: a) it is astonishingly difficult to gain an overall impression of parent opinion, as opposed to the views of minority groups; b) whenever parental opinion does emerge it is always strongly divided, often quite irreconcileably so.

Finally, how much sense does it make to talk of increasing or decreasing the power of teachers? We have already drawn a distinction between the power of the profession as a whole and the individual power of teachers, but here we are concerned with the power structure within a single school. For many years now the head has enjoyed, formally at least, a position of internal autocracy, however much this might be qualified by local tradition and personal idiosyncrasy. Recently, however, two factors have emerged to emphasize internal divisions in school staffs. One is the new hierarchical structure of schools, largely a function of increased school size, which has removed the head from direct contact with the work of junior assistants, and interposed various levels of intermediate command. The second, and it is obviously closely related to the first, is a growing consciousness among assistant teachers, perhaps especially among young teachers, of their special interests, and of consequent demands that their views should be represented in educational planning, and not just those of head-teachers and laymen. In higher education disaffected junior tutors have been prominent in arousing and directing criticism of and opposition to the establishment, and there are signs that a similar division between senior and junior members of staff is spreading to schools.

In all these cases we can see that the contemporary fashion for analysing social phenomena in terms of conflict between groups – social classes, generations, races, or in our case, teachers, parents, pupils – is seriously misleading because it diverts attention from foci of tension within the groups which may be more significant in providing clues to future developments than inter-group rivalries. It is precisely the fragmentation of the potentially powerful pressure groups of teachers and parents that justifies a fairly confident prediction that in the immediate future at least, any redistribution of power will involve a closer and more detailed supervision of schools by the constitutional authorities.

Of the developments we have examined so far few could not have been predicted in 1970. The power struggle has been a constant theme of educational history for 150 years at least, and although parent and pupil power have shown signs of challenging the twentieth-century monopoly of central and local government, even this has nineteenth-century precedents. Similarly, schools have been increasingly used as agents of social and political policy for a lengthy period; it is unsurprising that reaction should set in against the inflated aspirations and political totalitarianism of social engineers and advocates of community education.

But in higher education the 1970s have seen all predictions confounded and successive plans, of the government and others, reduced to nonsense by a quite unforseen reversal of well-established trends. In chapter 8 I spoke of the progressive acceptance in this country of the 'American' concept of higher education, arguing that the 1960s saw its victory over the traditional English or continental concept. Essentially the English have conceived higher education as a highly selective process, to be undertaken by relatively few students who propose to follow careers in scholarship or a limited range of professions. Other post-school training, however useful, enjoys lower status, a fact marked by the award of a qualification other than a degree. Americans, in contrast, have seen higher education as a more or less natural third stage following primary and secondary schools, taken by a large and increasing proportion of the population, with no English-style distinction between 'higher' and 'further' education. Writing in 1970 and reviewing the events of the previous twenty-five years it seemed reasonable to suppose that England was irrevocably committed to an American-type development, that higher education would continue to expand at an accelerating rate, increasingly becoming the normal completion of a young person's formal schooling. From the standpoint of 1975 the future looks far more problematical. What has happened to cause this change and to undermine the confident predictions of only five years ago?

The process began with the appointment of the James Committee in 1971 to investigate teacher training. The Committee reported early in 1972 and the general drift of its recommendations was that we should recognize the impossibility of providing once for all training at the commencement of a forty-year career, thinking rather of a less ambitious course of initial training, but supplementing it with far more comprehensive support for inexperienced teachers, together with a vastly expanded programme of recurrent in-service training. Some attention was also given to the professional isolation experienced by students at specialist teacher training colleges, and to the difficulty of transferring into and out of teacher training courses. Very wide approval was accorded to the general principles of the report, and indeed their logic was hard to dispute. The detailed proposals for implementing these principles were more controversial, but need not detain us here since they were almost entirely overtaken by events. By the time the Committee reported the government had seen that it was necessary to review the reform of teacher training as merely one part of a wider reorganization of higher education. Two factors were especially influential. Evidence was accumulating that we were over-producing teachers, and, if adjustments were made to recruitment, colleges of education would have unused accommodation and teaching power. This was a useful windfall, since demand for higher education was outstripping supply, especially in the arts and humanities, which were by and large the strongest academic sides of colleges of education. An undoubted added attraction was that unit costs for courses in colleges of education were very much lower than in polytechnics or universities, so that they provided an opportunity for relatively cheap expansion.

In December 1972 the D.E.S. produced its White Paper – *Education: A Framework for Expansion*. This was interesting as yet another attempt to impose a stratified system of higher education, with the third grade of institution providing diplomas of higher education rather than degrees. But, if events had followed the normal course of the 1950s and 1960s, this would soon have been written off as a reflex twitch of the conservative back bench, as the Dip. Tech. was a decade before. On the other hand the White Paper undeniably envisaged a massive expansion of higher education. Teacher training numbers were to be sharply reduced, three- and four-year courses being cut especially hard, while post-graduate entry was favoured. The available places, however were to be taken up by general higher education courses, with an emphasis upon the arts and humanities, and, either as independent institutions or by amalgamation with other colleges of education or with colleges of further education, some colleges were expected to increase their overall size as a result of their 'diversification'.

Up to this point, while colleges of education had suffered a demoralizing and upsetting period, higher education generally had flourished. Indeed universities and particularly polytechnics joined with enthusiasm in the criticism of colleges of education, realizing that the publicity given

171

to their shortcomings effectively distracted public attention from their own inadequacies, and averted the necessity for uncomfortable self-examination. Within a short time after the publication of the White Paper, however, its foundations began to appear very shaky. The first disturbing factor was an economic crisis of dimensions unprecedented since the 1930s. Building schemes were abandoned or postponed, staffing ratios re-examined, while the general economic gloom generated an unusually critical attitude towards public expenditure in general. On top of this, analysis of population trends made it clear that previous suppositions about population growth in the next decades were seriously at fault, and that the school population in the early 1980s was likely to be very much smaller than had been anticipated. The consequences for higher education in general and for teacher training in particular were obvious enough.

In all this there was nothing necessarily very new. Economic crises have blighted educational plans often enough, while governmental estimates of teacher requirements have invariably been wrong in the past; probably few expected them to be correct this time. There was, however, a new and disturbing phenomenon. Recruitment for higher education fell away sharply, teacher training being particularly badly affected. Even universities found their courses undersubscribed in certain areas while the imbalance of polytechnics towards the arts and humanities became ever more conspicuous. Among the courses worst affected were those for post-graduate teacher training, few colleges of education achieving their quota of students. All colleges found difficulty in obtaining candidates for their certificate and B.Ed. courses of the calibre they hoped for.

Why this should happen is not very clear. Certain special considerations apply to teacher recruitment. Much adverse publicity has been given in recent years to the pay and conditions of service of teachers, while the weaknesses of teacher training have been advertized to a public that knows nothing of the training of lawyers, engineers or doctors. But we seem to be dealing with a much wider phenomenon. Young people of undoubted academic quality are voting with their feet against full-time higher education, to enter employment, with or without part-time training. Perhaps they have realized that, except in a rather limited range of occupations, higher education conveys no particular career advantage and may even be a drawback. Perhaps the image of higher education has become tarnished of late by student unrest, the inadequacy of grants, and accounts of squalid living conditions. Perhaps the distinctly un-enthusiastic attitude of business and industry towards graduate employment, and their well-publicized preference for candidates who have learned in the army not to question the wisdom of their elders and betters, has a discouraging effect. It is too early yet to do more than speculate about the causes of this curious reversal of a long-standing trend, and too early even to be certain that it is a reversal and not a very temporary recession soon to be corrected. What is clear is that for a few years at least application for higher education will not be as automatic for duly qualified candidates as in the immediate past, so that universities, polytechnics and colleges will all face in varying degrees the dual pressures of financial stringency and competition for competent recruits.

CONCLUSION

In the introduction to this book I suggested that if the history of education is to achieve respectability it must aim to produce not merely an account of educational changes but also a body of explanatory theory, and that as a preparatory stage in this process it was worthwhile to pick out certain themes or processes of which such theories would have to take account. From the discussion in the preceding chapters is it possible to distinguish any such themes?

Perhaps the one which is most obvious is the progressive movement from a voluntary to a state system of education. For at least a quarter of a century after the idea of mass elementary education had been taken up there was no question of government intervention, and, indeed, early attempts at legislation were aimed at producing a system of schools based upon ecclesiastical parishes and under the supervision of the established Church. The forces which drove the government to undertake a direct measure of responsibility for education were clearly complex. Let us, examine, for example, some of the factors leading to the 1870 Act. The great lesson which was to be drawn from the period from 1800 to 1870 was that the provision of mass education was too great a task for voluntary effort, however devoted, and this was only underlined by the failure of 'Payment by Results' to make any impression upon the inadequacies revealed by the Newcastle Commission. At the same time the need for an extension of public elementary education was emphasized, on the one hand by the extension of the franchise in 1867 which raised fears of the results of handing power to an uneducated electorate, and on the other by alarm at the growth of large national units on the Continent of Europe, the recent successes of Prussia over Austria and France being in everyone's mind.

But the situation was not so simple as this for the extension of the franchise in 1867 and the Elementary Education Act of 1870 cannot be brought under the simple relationship of cause and effect. They were both symptoms, so to speak, of a movement towards democratizing society. Furthermore, they were the fruits of the much improved relationship between social classes which obtained in the 1860s as compared with the 1840s, for example – the University Extension

174

movement gained strength from the same reduction in inter-class tension.

Another complicating factor is that the Act of 1870 was not an isolated phenomenon. Government intervention in social problems began effectively in the 1830s and slowly gathered momentum and the Forster Act was only one of a number of important measures of social amelioration passed by a government which took a far more positive view of its role than any government would have done even twenty years earlier. To some extent this was due to the sheer pressure of facts; the Victorians were not inhuman and the repeated revelations, official and unofficial, of the ghastly conditions under which the poor lived and worked had a cumulative effect upon their consciences. But the assumptions upon which the laissez-faire view of a government's role was based were being assaulted on a philosophical level as well. In 1870 this assault was only beginning; individualism had been shown to be wanting but an alternative had not yet been offered which commanded general assent. By the 1880s this gap was being filled by writers such as T. H. Green and D. G. Ritchie. The title of one of Ritchie's books – *The Principles of State Intervention* – indicates the significance of this new school of thought.

It is not necessary to follow up the factors leading to state intervention in education any further; enough has been said to show that they were very complex and involve excursions into several branches of historical study. The fact is that at the beginning of our period education was a personal matter and the only official body which exercised, or claimed, any jurisdiction in the field was the Church. At the present time 95 children out of every 100 attend schools within the state system and even independent and private schools are subject to inspection and to a variety of regulations concerning their running and amenities. Recently there has been a marked increase in the amount of detailed control by the government over matters such as the organization of secondary education in which the Local Education Authorities have up to now enjoyed some freedom of manoeuvre. Here is one radical change for which the causes must be sought outside the normal boundaries of the history of education.

A somewhat similar group of questions is related to the internal politics of the school. Who determines what will be taught and what methods are to be used? At the beginning of the nineteenth century it was generally agreed that the syllabus and methods were to be imposed upon the school from outside. This was not surprising. Founders of charity schools and grammar schools had traditionally laid down fairly explicit instructions about the course which pupils were to follow, sometimes to the confusion of later headmasters who sought to modernize the curriculum. The managers of early nineteenth-century elementary schools were also often hampered by having to work through unintelligent and uneducated teachers, and one motive for the use of the monitorial system was that it was claimed that it worked effectively without the necessity for an expensively trained teacher. At precisely the same period Pestalozzi was seeking for a method of teaching which would work even in the hands of an ignorant peasant.

Under the Kay-Shuttleworth regime the degree of responsibility allowed to the teacher was increased and the tendency to allow the teacher progressively more authority over curricula and methods has continued until the last few years, when there appears to have been a distinct swing back towards the externally imposed schemes. There have been other periods when the tendency has been temporarily reversed, notably at the time of payment by results, and perhaps from about 1910 to 1914, but in general as the teacher's status has improved with better training and education, so his control over his work has increased. A factor which may be influential here, but which remains to be investigated, is the effect of the growing size of schools and the attendant stratification of staff.

The occasional reversals in the movement towards greater autonomy for the teacher raise the question of whether there is in the history of education anything similar to the 'long waves' which some authorities detect in economic history. This is a matter upon which the evidence at present allows for little more than speculation. There does, however, appear to be a noticeable alternation of what may be described as liberalism and reaction. If the Kay-Shuttleworth period was one of liberalism when there was a comparatively genial climate for experiment and innovation, it was followed by an indubitable reaction under 'payment by results'. The last years of the schools boards and the early years of Morant were 'liberal' but I seem to detect a reaction from about 1910, although this may be a local aberration. From the late 1960s the 'progressive' climate of the post-War period has encountered a very sharp reaction. It is interesting to notice that a feature common to all these periods of reaction is a reduction in the autonomy of the teacher. Other common features seem to be an emphasis upon social and political discipline as a motive for educational activity and a call for an increase in the cost-effectiveness of educational institutions. It is not particularly difficult to see some form of relationship between these features; one might perhaps describe a 'reactionary' period as one in which society asserted its right to control the educational system and to use it as an agency for socialization and vocational training. By contrast in the liberal periods schools follow a more 'child-centred' approach and there is a greater emphasis, both for teachers and children upon initiative and criticism.

One other important theme which forces itself upon the attention is the expansion of education which arises from internal pressure. It was in the 1870s that it first became apparent that the provision of universal elementary education was causing a demand for secondary education from those pupils who had gone as far as the elementary system would allow. Since then the same phenomenon has been influential on several occasions. In the 1920s it was largely responsible for the situation which brought about the Hadow reorganization; since the Second World War it has brought about, first a huge expansion of the demand for extended courses in secondary schools and more recently a correspondingly large development in higher education. This is interesting as being almost the only educational development for which one need not seek the cause outside the immediate field of educational history, but its repercussions range widely since the pressure upon facilities for higher education has led to a major shift in English attitudes towards universities, from what I have called in chapter 8 the 'European' to the 'American' approach. Here we have a case where essentially domestic developments within the educational system are causing social and political changes of some magnitude, and the end of the process is not yet clear since there must be some doubt about how the economy will cope with a substantial increase in the graduate population, especially since the great majority of the graduates are in subjects for which there is no very obvious demand.

I do not suppose that I have given an exhaustive list of the themes which historical theory must elucidate; these are merely a few suggestions which strike one after a fairly superficial glance at the development of English popular education. What is quite plain is that any attempt at explaining this development cannot be adequate if it is conducted from within the bounds of the history of education, as defined at the present time, but must relate educational changes in an integral manner with social, political and intellectual factors. It is not sufficient merely to set education against its contemporary background. A more dynamic approach is required which concerns itself seriously with the interaction between the educational system and the society of which it is one aspect.

GLOSSARY

BEVERIDGE REPORT. A report of 1942, prepared by Sir William Beveridge, which formed the basis of much post-War legislation related to the establishment of the welfare state.

THE BLACK PAPER(s). Collections of essays, published in 1969, 1970. In general they were critical of the 'progressive' position on educational matters.

BURNHAM COMMITTEE. The Burnham Committee, named after its first president, is a standing committee of representatives from local education authorities and teachers' associations which recommends scales of teachers' pay. The first Burnham Committee was formed in 1919.

CENTRAL SCHOOL. A post-primary school usually for selected pupils. Central schools were established between 1902 and 1944 by LEAs chiefly to provide for more able pupils who did not go to secondary (grammar) schools. They were classed as elementary schools.

CERTIFICATE OF SECONDARY EDUCATION. A school-leaving certificate designed to be at a standard slightly below the 'ordinary' level of the GCE. It is organized on a regional basis and teachers are represented on the regional committees. The CSE was recommended by the Beloe Committee, which reported in 1960.

CHARTISM. A working-class political movement, active c. 1838–48 which demanded the acceptance by the government of a 'charter' of six points, including manhood suffrage and payment of MPs. The movement tended to fall into two wings, referred to as 'moral force' and 'physical force' chartists, because of the methods of agitation which they favoured.

CIRCULAR 10/65. A circular from the Department of Education and Science to local education authorities setting out the government's policy with respect to the abolition of selection and the move towards comprehensive secondary education.

COCKERTON JUDGMENT. A decision by an official auditor in 1899 that the London School Board was acting illegally in spending public money on education beyond the elementary stage. It had the effect of preventing school boards from developing higher grade schools.

COMPREHENSION. A system by which all pupils of secondary age in a school area attend the same school. To be contrasted with the 'tripartite' system or 'selection'.

CONTINUATION SCHOOL. Proposals have frequently been made, notably by the Fisher Act of 1918, that part-time education be provided for pupils who leave school at the minimum leaving age. Such education is referred to as 'continuative' schooling, and the schools as 'continuation' schools.

DALTON PLAN. A system by which pupils are given assignments of work for a week or month which they are free to organize as they wish. The plan is credited to the work of Helen Parkhurst at Dalton High School, Massachusetts.

DAME SCHOOLS. Small schools for young children run by women in the eighteenth and nineteenth century, often as a supplement to other activities. Slightly more pretentious schools were called 'common day' schools.

FABIAN SOCIETY. A society established in 1883 to advocate the reform of society on evolutionary lines. Members included Sidney and Beatrice Webb, Bernard Shaw and G. D. H. Cole.

FRIENDLY SOCIETIES. Societies for mutual assistance founded by members of the working class in large numbers in the late eighteenth and nineteenth centuries.

'GEDDES AXE'. A committee established under the chairmanship of Sir Eric Geddes in 1921, to consider government economies in the first of the inter-War slumps. Many of the provisions of the 'Fisher' Act of 1918 were made inoperative by this slump.

GENERAL CERTIFICATE OF EDUCATION. In 1951 the General School Certificate and Higher School Certificate (q.v.) were replaced by the GCE which is taken at 'ordinary', 'advanced' and 'scholarship' level. 'Ordinary' or O levels are taken at about the age of sixteen. 'Advanced' or A levels are taken after two years further work in the sixth form at eighteen.

GENERAL SCHOOL CERTIFICATE. Instituted in 1917, this was an examination for grammar school pupils, taken at about the age of sixteen years. The *Higher School Certificate* was taken at eighteen years.

HER MAJESTY'S INSPECTORS (HMI). Government inspectors of schools, first appointed in 1839 to supervise elementary schools which received government grant.

HIGHER SCHOOL CERTIFICATE – see *General School Certificate*.

LEICESTERSHIRE PLAN. A scheme proposed in 1957 to reorganize secondary education in Leicestershire. It is based largely upon a process of self-selection. All children go to a high school at ten, and can choose to go to a grammar school at thirteen if they wish.

MAY COMMITTEE. A committee under Sir George May which, in 1931, advised the Chancellor of the Exchequer on government economies. So far as education was concerned the chief economies were that teachers' salaries were cut by 10 per cent, building was suspended, and 'free' places were changed to 'special' places which were geared to parental income.

Glossary

OBJECTIVE TESTS. Tests which are designed to exclude the subjective element which enters into the marking of answers of the essay type.

OXFORD AND CAMBRIDGE LOCAL EXAMINATIONS. School-leaving examinations held in local centres throughout the country under the aegis of the universities. Founded in 1858 they were forerunners of the General School Certificate.

PAYMENT BY RESULTS. A system for assessing the payment of government grant to elementary schools which was introduced by the Revised Code of 1862 and continued with modifications until 1897. Grant was based upon: (a) attendance for a stipulated number of half days; (b) individual examinations of pupils in the three 'R's, (c) certain extra payments which varied from time to time.

PROJECTS, PROJECT METHOD. A method of teaching which involves the pupil in independent enquiry into a relatively large field of work. Projects are often set to groups of pupils rather than to individuals.

PUBLIC SCHOOL. Originally a term which referred to nine large, chiefly boarding, schools, including Eton, Harrow, Winchester, and Rugby. Later a more general term referring to independent non-profit-making secondary schools, particularly those which are members of the Headmasters' Conference.

RAGGED SCHOOLS. Schools for very poor children established in the nineteenth century when it became apparent that such children were often excluded from existing schools because of their ragged clothing and appearance.

RUSKIN COLLEGE. An adult college founded in 1899 for working-class students. In 1910 it came under the control of the trades unions.

SCIENCE AND ART DEPARTMENT. A government department, established in 1853, following the Great Exhibition of 1851, to encourage the teaching of science and technology. From 1859 it made grants to teachers on a payment by results basis. In 1899 it was merged with the Board of Education.

SETTING – see *Streaming*.

SOCIETY FOR PROMOTING CHRISTIAN KNOWLEDGE (SPCK). A society formed in 1698 which, in the early eighteenth century, was very active in establishing charity schools for the education of the poor.

STREAMING. The practice of placing in the same class pupils of approximately the same ability. The effects of streaming, especially in primary schools, have been the subject of much dispute during the late 1960s. Where pupils move from group to group for different subjects the system is called *setting*.

TRIPARTITE SYSTEM. The scheme by which, after the 1944 Act, secondary education in England and Wales was organized on a basis of grammar schools, secondary technical schools and secondary modern schools. The scheme is generally attributed to the Norwood Report of 1943, but the idea that secondary education should be divided into three strata can be traced back at least to the 1840s.

180

WEAVER REPORT. Published in 1966, it examined the status of colleges of education and advocated that they should enjoy a greater measure of autonomy.

WORKERS' EDUCATIONAL ASSOCIATION (WEA). An association formed in 1903 to further the adult education of the working class by co-ordinating the efforts of trades unions, the universities and the co-operative movement.

FURTHER READING

GENERAL HISTORIES OF EDUCATION

Adamson, J. W. *English Education, 1789–1902*. Cambridge, 1930.

Armytage, W. H. G. *Four Hundred Years of English Education*. Cambridge, 1964.

Barnard, H. C. *A History of English Education from 1760*. London, 1961.

Boyd, W. *A History of Western Education*. Black, 1966.

Curtis, S. J. *History of Education in Great Britain*. U.T.P., 1967.

and Boultwood, M.E.A. *A Short History of Educational Ideas*. U.T.P. 1953.

Maclure, J. S. *Educational Documents, 1816–1963*. Methuen, 1965.

Peterson, A. D. C. *A Hundred Years of Education*. Duckworth, 1960.

Simon, B. *Studies in the History of Education, 1780–1870*. Lawrence and Wishart, 1960.

Education and the Labour Movement, 1870–1920. Lawrence and Wishart, 1965.

WORKS ON SPECIFIC ASPECTS OF EDUCATION

Archer, R. L. *Secondary Education in the Nineteenth Century*. Cambridge, 1921.

Argles, M. *South Kensington to Robbins*. Longmans, 1964.

Banks, O. *Parity and Prestige in English Secondary Education*. Routledge and Kegan Paul, 1955.

Bernbaum, G. *Social Change and the Schools*. Routledge and Kegan Paul, 1967.

Burgess, H. J. *Enterprise in Education*. SPCK, 1958.

Cruikshank, M. *Church and State in English Education*. Macmillan, 1964.

Curtis, S. J. *Education in Britain since 1900*. London, 1952.

Dobbs, A. E. *Education and Social Movements, 1780–1850*. Longmans, 1919.

Eaglesham, E. C. *From School Board to Local Authority*. Routledge and Kegan Paul, 1956.

The Foundations of Twentieth Century English Education. Routledge and Kegan Paul, 1968.

Graves, J. *Policy and Progress in Secondary Education*. Nelson, 1943.

Lester-Smith, W. O. *To Whom do Schools Belong?* Blackwell, 1945.

Lowndes, G. A. N. *The Silent Social Revolution*. Oxford, second edition, 1969.

Rubinstein, D. and Simon, B. *The Evolution of the Comprehensive School, 1926–1966*. Routledge and Kegan Paul, 1969.

Skidelsky, R. *English Progressive Schools*. Pelican, 1969.

Sneyd-Kinnersley, E. M. *H.M.I.* Macmillan, 1913.

Stewart, W. A. C. and McCann, W. P. *The Educational Innovators*. 2 volumes, Macmillan, 1968.

Sturt, M. *The Education of the People*. Routledge and Kegan Paul, 1967.

WORKS ON TOPICS RELATED TO EDUCATION

Altick, R. D. *The English Common Reader*. Chicago, 1957.

Briggs, A. *The Age of Improvement*. Longmans, 1959.

Bullock, A. and Shock, M. *The Liberal Tradition*. Black, 1956.

Engels, F. *The Condition of the Working Class in England in 1848*. Allen and Unwin, 1892.

George, M. D. *England in Transition*. Pelican, 1953.

Gosse, E. *Father and Son*. Penguin, 1949.

Hammond, J. L., and B. *The Age of the Chartists*. Longmans, 1930.
The Skilled Labourer, 1760–1932. Longmans, 1919.

Hewitt, M. *Wives and Mothers in Victorian Industry*. Rockliffe, 1958.

Hobsbawm, E. J. *Industry and Empire*. Weidenfeld and Nicolson, 1968.

Kitson-Clark, G. *The Making of Victorian England*. Macmillan, 1962.

Tawney, R. H. *The Radical Tradition*. Pelican, 1966.

Thompson, E. P. *The Making of the English Working Class*. Gollancz, 1963.

Wearmouth, R. F. *Some Working Class Movements of the Nineteenth Century*. Epworth, 1948.

Webb, R. K. *The British Working Class Reader, 1790–1848*. Allen and Unwin, 1955.

Young, G. M. (ed.). *Early Victorian England*. Oxford, 1934.

RECENT PUBLICATIONS

Faure, E. *Learning to Be*. UNESCO/Harrap, 1972.

Husen, T. *The Learning Society*. Methuen, 1974.

Illich, I. *De-Schooling Society*. Calder and Boyars, 1971.

Jencks, C. *Inequality*. Penguin, 1975.

Keddie, N. *Tinker, Tailor, The Myth of Cultural Deprivation*. Penguin, 1973.

Lawson, J. and Silver, H. *A Social History of Education in England*. Methuen, 1973.

Midwinter, E. *Patterns of Community Education*. Ward Lock, 1973.

Musgrove, F. *Patterns of Power and Authority in English Education*. Methuen, 1971.

Rubinstein, D. and Stoneman, C. S. *Education for Democracy*. Penguin, 1970.

Wardle, D. *The Rise of the Schooled Society*. Routledge and Kegan Paul, 1974.

CHRONOLOGICAL TABLE

Educational events		General historical events	
		1776	Declaration of Independence by USA
1780	Establishment of Sunday schools by Raikes		
		1789	Start of French Revolution
		1793	Execution of Louis XVI Britain and France at war Repression of 'Jacobins' in England
		1799	Political associations banned Combination Acts
1810	British and Foreign School Society		
1811	National Society	1811	'Luddism' and other social and political unrest
		1819	'Peterloo'
1820s	Mechanics institutes Society for the Diffusion of Useful Knowledge University College London	1820s	'Liberal Toryism', work of Peel, Huskisson, Canning, Robinson Reform of penal code; removal of restrictions upon Dissenters and Catholics; repeal of Combination Acts
1828	Arnold at Rugby		
		1830s	Parliamentary reform 1832 followed by Liberal government – breach in laissez-faire e.g. Factory Act 1833 Abolition of Slavery 1834
1833	Treasury grant for school building		

184

Poor Law 1834
Municipal Reform 1835

1838–48 Chartism; agitation for repeal of Corn Laws; Irish famine; economic distress

1839 Committee of Privy Council for Education, Sir James Kay-Shuttleworth secretary

1840s Establishment of proprietorial secondary schools

1846 Pupil-teacher system

1848 Year of revolution in Europe

1850s Improvement in economic position and decline in social and political tension

1851 Great Exhibition

1853 Science and Art Department

1854–6 Crimean War

1856 Education Department established

1858 Oxford and Cambridge 'Local' examinations

1859 Publication of *Origin of Species*

1861–5 American Civil War

1861 Newcastle Commission

1862 Revised Code – payment by results

1864 Clarendon Commission

1866 Austro-Prussian War

1868 Taunton Commission

1867 Parliamentary Reform Act

Chronological table

1870	'Forster' Education Act – establishment of school boards	1870	Franco-Prussian War – foundation of Germany
			Beginning of 'great depression' in Britain
	Sandon's Act (1876) and Mundella's Act (1880) make education compulsory		
	Higher grade schools appear from *c.* 1878		
	Establishment of 'Municipal Universities'		
		1884	Third Parliamentary Reform Act – Manhood suffrage established
1888	Cross Commission		
		1889	County Councils established
1890	Day training colleges in universities		
1893	Free elementary education		
1895	Bryce Commission		
1899	Board of Education established		
		1899–1902	Boer War
1902	'Balfour' Education Act – local education authorities established		
1905	*Handbook of Suggestions for Teachers*	1905	Liberal government returned
1906	School meals		
1907	Medical inspection 'Free place' regulations		
1908	Bursary system for teacher training Boy Scouts formed	1908	Old age pensions Children's Act
1910	Girl Guides		

186

		1911	National Health insurance
		1914–18	First World War
		1916	Ministry of Reconstruction Labour party adopts policy of 'secondary education for all'
		1917	Ministry of Labour
1918	'Fisher' Education Act	1918	Parliamentary suffrage for some women
1919	Burnham Committee	1919	Ministry of Health
1920	Teachers' superannuation	1920	Unemployment Insurance Act
		1922	'Geddes Axe'
1926	Hadow Report – 'Education of the Adolescent'	1926	General Strike
		1931	Financial crisis May Committee
1932	'Special' places replace 'free' places Teachers' salaries reduced		
		1933	Hitler in power in Germany
1938	Spens Report	1939–45	Second World War
		1942	Beveridge Report
1943	Norwood Report – basis for application of 1944 Act to secondary education		
1944	'Butler' Education Act Ministry of Education replaces Board of Education		
		1945	Labour party in power
		1947	Coal industry nationalized

		1948	National Health Service Railways nationalized
		1949	Iron and steel industries nationalized
		1950	Legal Aid established
1951	General Certificate of Education instituted	1951	Conservative party in power
		1952	First 'H' bomb exploded
1955	Duke of Edinburgh's Award Scheme		
		1956	First Aldermaston March
1957	Leicestershire plan proposed	1957	First Sputnik flight
		1958	Racial disturbances in London and Nottingham
1959	Crowther Report		
1960	Beloe Report on secondary school examinations		
1961	onwards Establishment of 'new' universities		
1963	Newsom Report Robbins Report First teaching machines in English schools		
1964	Announcement of proposed raising of school-leaving age to 16 Ministry of Education becomes Department of Education and Science Schools' Council instituted	1964	Labour government returned Ministry of Technology formed
1965	Certificate of Secondary Education (CSE) instituted Circular 10/65 Training colleges renamed colleges of education	1965	Suspension of death penalty
1966	Proposal to establish polytechnics		

	Weaver Report on Government of Colleges of Education		
1967	Plowden Report		
	Proposal to establish Open University		
1968	Dainton Report on flow of students into science and technology	1968	Drastic cuts in public expenditure
	Student unrest becomes a public issue		
	Raising of school-leaving age deferred from 1971 to 1973		
1969	Black Paper		
1970	Circular 10/70	1970	Conservative government elected
1971	James Report		
1972	White Paper – *A Framework for Expansion*		
1973	Circular 7/73		
	Raising of school-leaving age to 16 years		
1974	Decline in recruitment affects plans for higher education	1974	Financial crisis affects public expenditure
	Bullock Report		Labour government elected
	Houghton Report		
	Circular 4/74		
1974	Reorganization of teacher training		
	William Tyndale case	1975	Financial crisis continues

189

INDEX

Index

Index